Devotional Activism

Other Books of Interest from St. Augustine's Press

D. Q. McInerny, *Being Philosophical*

Anne Drury Hall, *Where the Muses Still Haunt: The Second Reading*

Michael Franz (editor), *Eric Voegelin's Late Meditations and Essays: Critical Commentary Companions*

David Ramsay Steele, *The Conquistador with His Pants Down: David Ramsay Steele's Legendary Lost Lectures*

Cristian Mendoza and Lluís Clavell, *Communication Culture in a Digital Age: Being Seriously Relational*

Francisco Insa, *The Formation of Affectivity: A Christian Approach*

Marvin R. O'Connell, *Telling Stories that Matter: Memoirs and Essays*

Josef Pieper, *Traditional Truth, Poetry, Sacrament: For My Mother, on her 70th Birthday*

Pete Fraser, *Twelve Films about Love and Heaven*

Peter Kreeft, *Ha!: A Christian Philosophy of Humor*

Gabriele Kuby, *The Abandoned Generation*

David Lowenthal, *Slave State: Rereading Orwell's 1984*

Gene Fendt, *Camus' Plague: Myth for Our World*

Nalin Ranasinghe, *The Confessions of Odysseus*

John Poch, *God's Poems: The Beauty of Poetry and Christian Imagination*

Bartholomew of the Martyrs, O.P., *Stimulus Pastorum: A Charge to Pastors*

Maurice Ashley Agbaw-Ebai, *The Essential Supernatural: A Dialogical Study in Kierkegaard and Blondel*

Maurice Ashley Agbaw-Ebai, *Light of Reason, Light of Faith: Joseph Ratzinger and the German Enlightenment*

Stanley Rosen, *The Language of Love: An Interpretation of Plato's Phaedrus*

Leon J. Podles, *Losing the Good Portion: Why Men Are Alienated from Christianity*

Winston Churchill, *The River War*

Devotional Activism

Public Religion, Innovation and Culture in the Nineteenth Century

Richard Schaefer

St. Augustine's Press

South Bend, Indiana

Manufactured in the United States of America.

1 2 3 4 5 6   29 28 27 26 25 24

Library of Congress Control Number: 2023947644

Paperback ISBN: 978-1-58731-187-1
Ebook ISBN: 978-158731-188-8

Portions of chapter one were published previously in *Journal of Religion and Society*. Portions of chapter two were published in *Nineteenth Century Contexts*. A previous version of chapter three was published in *First World War Studies*, and chapter four was previously published in *Zygon: Journal of Religion and Science*. A version of chapter five was previously published in *Brentano Studien*. The author wishes to thank the publishers for permission to republish.

∞ The paper used in this publication meets the minimum requirements of the American National Standard for Information Sciences – Permanence of Paper for Printed Materials, ANSI Z39.48-1984.

St. Augustine's Press
www.staugustine.net

For Amy, Max, and Kate, who carry my heart.

Table of Contents

INTRODUCTION
PUBLIC RELIGION, INNOVATION
AND CULTURE

In the mid-1990s, when I was in my first year at graduate school, I was lucky enough to be invited to a post-conference dinner with the keynote speaker and some faculty. It was an honor, and I was a little nervous, having not yet quite convinced myself that I belonged with all of these prestigious scholars. Just as I was starting to feel a little more comfortable with myself and my surroundings, a senior professor whom I had been eager to meet—a person of some renown—flopped in her chair and started complaining to the faculty at the table about the generally poor caliber of graduate students in recent years. They were, in her judgment, a frustrating combination of timid and boring, interested only in recycling old ideas. I tried as best I could, to blend into the background as others nodded knowingly, only to have her turn to me after a few moments and ask me who I was and "what I do." It was rude. I knew it then and I know it now, but even today I can still remember how frightened and intimidated I was at that moment. What could I say that would sound impressive and single me out as neither timid nor boring? I did the only thing I have ever known how to do—I was honest. I told her that my interest was religion. She nodded blankly, and turned to engage someone else in conversation. I didn't even merit an eye-roll, let alone a rejoinder. I had seen that look before, and I have seen it since. It lives in the academy. It is a look that says, without ever really saying so, religion is stupid, an atavistic holdover from a less enlightened age, an affront, an embarrassment, an impediment to serious thought, and those who take it seriously give it too much credence, when the best thing to do would be to let it wither and die.

As anyone reading this book will probably already know, much has changed since then. Indeed, to everyone's surprise, there has been a surge of interest in religion in the academy in the last twenty years, with a steady stream of books, blogs, conferences, and journals all declaring that religion "was back." In 2006, the editors of the *Journal of the American Academy of Religion* declared that "never in the JAAR's history has religion been so prominent a factor in the public consciousness as it is today."[1] And in 2009, more historians identified religion as a research interest than any other sub-field.[2] (*Imagine my surprise when the same senior professor went on at length several years later on the need to understand better the relevance of religion to a range of issues!*) This surge of interest did not come entirely out of the blue, of course. Even while I was still in graduate school, some of the more mystical strains of postmodern theorizing hinted at new possibilities for thinking about religion. Although seemingly paradoxical, given the overall postmodern rejection of stable foundations and authoritative master narratives, encounters with figures like Walter Benjamin and Emmanuel Levinas prompted some to rethink the significance of religion, if in admittedly unorthodox ways. John Caputo, Gianni Vattimo, Slavoj Žižek, and even Jacques Derrida are just some of the theorists who suggested that religion might have untapped potential for addressing the challenges of advanced industrial, technological societies. Though their talk of "religion without religion" would certainly have confused the average Churchgoer, their renewed interest in religion was a breath of fresh air and an impetus to the broader rethinking of religion taking place today in the academy. At the very least, these efforts helped lift the taboo that prevented so many scholars from taking religion seriously at all for so long.

The irony of this new state of affairs was not lost on Peter Berger, one of the major proponents of the secularization thesis in the 1960s.[3] In 1999,

---

1   "Editor's Note," *Journal of the American Academy of Religion* 74:1 (March 2006): 1.

2   Robert B. Townshend, "A New-Found Religion? The Field Surges Among AHA Members," in *Perspectives on History* 47 (December 2009).

3   The irony was also not lost on René Girard, who observes: "The Christian religion cannot even be mentioned in certain settings, or it can only be discussed in order to keep it under control, keep it in check, on the pretext that there is nothing positive in it, indeed on the grounds that it bears prime and sole responsibility for the horrors of the modern world. And it seems to me that there is a remarkable irony in the fact that the people who completely abandoned this tradition are now beginning to take a fresh interest in these problems—especially the most influential sector of the avant garde...." See Gianni

Berger openly reversed his previous position and declared that a "whole body of literature by historians and social scientists loosely labeled 'secularization theory' ... [was] essentially mistaken." In contrast with expectations, societal modernization had not led to a large-scale waning of religion, and "[t]he world today ... is as furiously religious as it ever was, and in some places more so than ever."[4] The main problem, according to Berger, had been parochialism, and failing to see that trends in Western Europe that were taken as the norm actually constituted an exception to what was happening globally. Because they lacked a truly global perspective on religion, scholars failed to see the dynamic "interplay between secularizing and counter-secularizing forces." But the problem was also elitism: "There exists an international subculture composed of people with Western-type higher education, especially in the humanities and social sciences, that is indeed secularized. This subculture is the principal 'carrier' of progressive, Enlightened beliefs and values. While its members are relatively thin on the ground, they are very influential, as they control the institutions that provide the 'official' definitions of reality, notably the educational system, the media of mass communication, and the higher reaches of the legal system. They are remarkably similar all over the world today, as they have been for a long time (though, as we have seen, there are also defectors from this subculture, especially in the Muslim countries)."[5] Cutting across national boundaries, this "globalized elite culture" simply had no interest in "religious upsurges ... [of] a strongly populist character," having decided in advance that these belonged on the wrong side of history. This, as much as anything else, was responsible for the poor state of research into religion. Whether members of the subculture Berger describes have changed their minds about the desirability of "progressive, Enlightened beliefs and values" is doubtful. What is certain, however, is that scholars across numerous disciplines, including history, have become strongly interested in populist upsurges of religion, and the essays collected here contribute to that literature. Written over the last ten years,

---

Vattimo and René Girard, *Christianity, Truth, and Weakening Faith: A Dialogue* (Columbia UP, 2010), 66.

4   Peter Berger, *The Descularization of the World: Resurgent Religion and World Politics* (Eerdman's Publishing Company, 1999), 2.

5   Ibid., 10.

they leverage new research on the limits and possibilities of secularization to explore the intersection of religion with politics and culture.

One of the most important books to reframe how we approach this intersection has been José Casanova's *Public Religions in the Modern World*. In it, he analyzes a set of religious movements from the 1980s and tenders the thesis that "we are witnessing the 'deprivatization' of religion." This consisted, quite simply, of "religious traditions throughout the world ... refusing to accept the marginal and privatized role which theories of modernity as well as theories of secularization had reserved for them." That did not mean that secularization itself "was, or is, a myth," since "the thesis of the differentiation and emancipation of the secular spheres from religious institutions and norms, remains valid." What was decidedly new was religion's determination to "participate in the very struggles to define and set the modern boundaries between the private and public spheres, between system and life-world, between legality and morality, between individual and society, between family, civil society, and state, between nations, states, civilizations, and the world system." Rather than accept the right of the state to enforce a particular vision of its proper role, what defines public religion in the modern world is its willingness to "rais[e] questions publicly about the autonomous pretensions of the differentiated [social] spheres to function without regard to moral norms or human considerations."[6] Of course, secularization has been taken to mean many things, as Casanova notes. Originally, it was used to describe the transfer of property from ecclesiastical to secular ownership. Only later was it used to describe: 1) a process of societal modernization that placed religion into new (and subordinate) relations with other spheres of social activity, such as politics, economics, art, etc., and 2) a widespread and largely elite belief about the course of history, namely, that religion was no longer (and would no longer be) of central significance in the life of the great majority of people who had thus become "modernized."[7] This latter

6   José Casanova, *Public Religions in the Modern World* (Chicago: University of Chicago Press, 1994).

7   One result of renewed interest in religion has been a proliferation of attempts to parse and categorize the varieties of secularization. For more see Craig Calhoun, Mark Juergensmeyer, and Jonathan VanAntwerpen, *Rethinking Secularism* (New York: Oxford UP, 2011).

use of secularization, though rooted in empirical observations about the dynamics of societal modernization, was no less infused with a metaphysics of its own—a conviction about the course of history that was not purely the result of empirical evidence. History—both how it is written and how it is imagined—has been a crucial element in how we think about religion, and religion, by the same token, served as a structuring element in the emergence of modern historical consciousness. As a "master narrative" of history, secularization does not just take place in time, but delimits what we can know in time, serving as an axis for discriminating modern from pre-modern forms of life and helping thus to establish the formal conditions for measuring historical progress.[8]

One of the themes taken up in the essays collected here is public religion, and the role of Catholicism in challenging the normative impetus of a singular view of secularization as societal modernization. Beginning with the Enlightenment, Catholicism became iconic of the backwards religious "other" who failed to adapt to the needs of the present.[9] And yet, this image clashes with the fact that, throughout the nineteenth century, Catholics demonstrated a growing readiness to undertake public, and even political, action in the name of the faith. Catholics fought with others over education, politics, and the rights of workers and religious minorities, and they waged a campaign to secure a morally appropriate Catholic voice in popular literature and the press.[10] Catholics were enlisted to participate in petition writing campaigns and formed blocs of elected delegates, as during the revolutions of 1848. They were also, on extreme occasions, willing to confront the state head-on, as in the controversy over the arrest of the archbishop of Cologne in 1838. In all of these instances, and many more, what needs to be emphasized is how these efforts consisted of a set of more or less ad hoc strategies for competing with the welter of new ideas and rapidly changing circumstances. It was not the result of a coordinated plan on the part of

---

8 Jeffrey Cox, "Secularization and Other Master Narratives of Religion in Modern Europe," in *Kirchliche Zeitgeschichte* 14 (2001).

9 For more on how Protestant Christianity became the model for what all religions should be, see Brent Nongbri, *Before Religion. A History of a Modern Concept* (New Haven: Yale University Press, 2015).

10 Margaret Stieg Dalton, *Catholicism, Popular Culture, and the Arts in Germany, 1880–1933* (University of Notre Dame Press, 2005).

the Church hierarchy, who struggled at times to corral this surge in popular sentiment.[11] Building on Casanova's research into public religion, I show that the Catholic rejoinder to modernization offers important insights into the fecundity of religion for mustering new avenues of political self-assertion.

A second, and related, theme explored in these essays involves religion as an impetus for innovation.[12] In the terms set by the master narrative of secularization, religion only ever serves as the counterpoint to progress, the point of departure for new discoveries in science, art, and politics. Viewed in this way, how could it ever be anything other than a brake on innovation? Part of the problem, of course, is that those promoting innovations in religion overwhelmingly tend to deny that they are doing so. The rhetoric of return," "revival," and "reformation" makes it hard to see how some of these events might really be better seen as instances of "the invention of tradition."[13] But as the essays here show, the impulse towards revival is never just a simple desire to return to the past, involving as it does more complex strategies for making the past ready to "fit" into the present. Though it is frequently overlooked and even denied, innovation might be seen to run to the very core of religion, especially if one is open to seeing the conflict between orthodoxy and apostasy as more of a dialectic than a strictly agonistic contest. There is no denying how the great majority of religious communities claim definitive positions as religious truth, and make affirming fidelity to those "beliefs" the condition for membership in these communities. But as the history of religion so clearly shows, this hardly seems to have blunted religion's capacity for self-expression. One might even say it has encouraged it. The deeper vitality of religions is precisely their capacity to generate disagreement alongside belief, which conduces as much to creativity and dissent, as to rigid assertions of orthodoxy. Religion is never a

11 Mary Heimann "Catholic Revivalism in worship and devotion" in *The Cambridge History of Christianity: Volume 8, World Christianities c.1815–c.1914*, eds. Sheridan Gilley and Brian Stanley (New York: Cambridge University Press, 2006): 70–83.

12 Donald A. Yerxa, *Religion and Innovation. Antagonists or Partners?* (Bloomsbury, 2015).

13 Eric Hobsbawm and Terence Ranger, eds., *The Invention of Tradition* (New York: Cambridge University Press, 1983).

static "thing" but a set of dynamic ideas and practices, constantly shaping and being shaped by circumstances. This would seem like something that "goes without saying," but it needs to be stressed, since one thing that supporters and detractors of religion alike seem to share is a stubborn preference for talking about religion as if it were something solid, stable, and immune to change. It is not hard to understand why. For the religious, religion consists of opening oneself to a transcendent order, one that stands outside of ordinary time (though time might be mobilized in the service of revelation, as it is in Christianity). For critics, religion consists of habits, prejudices, superstitions, and other holdovers from a pre-critical time, one that stands opposed to reason and progress.[14] Whatever one might want to say in defense of either view, and for whatever reason, both are patently falsifiable as statements about the course of history. Things change, and that includes religion. The trick is to understand how and when this change is denied, repressed, masked, or otherwise assimilated to structures of permanence, and in the service of what goals. And the challenge is to develop a new and more supple approach to how religious convictions and practices unfold every day in changing circumstances.

The third and final theme taken up in this volume involves taking stock of the tendency to reduce religion to culture. As an instrument for interpreting human affairs, culture stresses the contingency of religious practice over the formal rules of doctrine and membership, and elevates local meaning-production over the prescriptive force of institutional authorities. Part of the broader shift away from Marxian and other categories of social analysis, the turn to culture has enabled scholars to think more

14 There is, of course, a wide variety of different ideas about what constitutes progress in history. At the most basic level, one would want to distinguish between utopian visions that posit arriving at an ideal set of circumstances in history (or beyond), and limitless material, scientific, technological improvement unconnected from a final set of circumstances. Such visions fall on a wide spectrum of the religious/secular, and there is a rich literature debating the degree to which they might be mutually imbricated in various ways. For the most part, when I refer to progress, I do so to capture the various ways this is imagined as involving a necessary and inevitable decline in the relevance of religion for navigating issues in society and politics. But I qualify this usage where necessary, as in my treatment of A. D. White and Franz Brentano.

deeply about agency, about how people creatively inhabit the worlds that they make and remake in the course of their lives. Though perhaps articulated most compellingly by anthropologists, culture is a *topos* that cuts across various academic interests and disciplinary boundaries. In the field of history, culture has helped historians uncover the rich texture of meaning in local, popular practices like carnivals, pilgrimages, and even pornography. It has helped move historians away from more arid analyses of society and structure into the richer dimensions of *mentalités* and the contingency of experience. And yet, in spite of the fact that cultural analysis shows how the world is a dynamic place, there is still a tendency to blunt what is perhaps singular and unique about religion by reducing it to "culture" as a kind of trans-historical essence. It is a tendency that manifests itself in the desire to see every conflict involving religion as a chapter in the perennial "culture wars," and in the prevalence of what Mahmood Mamdani has dubbed "culture talk," which "assumes that every culture has a tangible essence that defines it, and then explains politics as a consequence of that essence." In the hands of policy analysts and media commentators, culture talk is a popular way of framing connections between geo-politics and religion to the broader public. It presents religion as the unreflective core of culture, as the unquestioned repository of motives and meanings that drive action. In discussions of Islam, culture is presented as the "lifeless custom of an antique people who inhabit antique lands." It is presented as "habit ... some kind of instinctive activity with rules that are inscribed in early founding texts, usually religious, and mummified in early artifacts."[15] Of course, Mamdani is very careful to distinguish between "the culture studied by anthropologists," which is "face-to-face, intimate, local, and lived," and "talk of culture [that] ... comes in large geo-packages." That said, historians are not immune to the lure of culture talk, and there is a powerful tendency within the profession to see religion as really "about something else," rather than take at face value what religious actors themselves claim to be doing.[16] This is due in part, no doubt, to a desire to hew

15   Mahmood Mamdani, *Good Muslim, Bad Muslim: America, the Cold War, and the Roots of Terror* (New York: Doubleday, 2005), 18.
16   Robert Laurence Moore, *Touchdown Jesus: The Mixing of Sacred and Secular in American History* (Louisville: Westminster, 2003).

8

to a methodological atheism, a desire, in other words, to shield oneself from any hint of being influenced by the truth content of religious beliefs. But as Alister Chapman, John Coffey, and Brad Gregory observe, historians still overwhelmingly prefer "to explain religious beliefs as a mask for more fundamental social, economic, or political interests" at the cost of "seeing things their way."[17]

To see religion as culture means presenting it as the root source of meaning, a bulwark against anxiety and rootlessness. And yet, as I've already intimated, there is an important sense in which religion itself conduces to innovation, and even instability.[18] By calling people to do more, and be more—to "self-transcendence" as Hans Joas calls it—religion helps reimagine the coordinates of experience. Indeed, as Joas puts it, religious "[f]aith does not simply emanate from either rousing or anxious experiences," but "articulates such experiences of self-transcendence" in ways that are unavailable to nonbelievers.[19] This experience of a new reality is as much the goal as the ground of religion, and it is poorly grasped as culture, since even to strive for such an experience means calling into question existing interpretive patterns and habits of mind. Religion doesn't just supply answers, it asks questions, and those who immerse themselves in it often experience a deeper kind of questioning than is available in other spheres of life. What happens when there are no answers, but the questions remain? One of the things that has yet to be sufficiently considered, it seems to me, is how

17 Alister Chapman, John Coffey, and Brad S. Gregory, eds., *Seeing Things Their Way: Intellectual History and the Return of Religion* (South Bend: University of Notre Dame Press, 2009), 11.

18 Years ago, Dominick LaCapra challenged the notion that culture was an inherently stable entity by pointing to the complex and contestatory tendencies at work in and between levels of high, popular, and mass culture. This is an issue that is no less relevant when studying religion. See Dominick LaCapra, "Is Everyone a Mentalité Case? Transference and the 'Culture' Concept," in *History & Criticism* (Ithaca: Cornell University Press, 1985): 71–94. For a collection of essays that also subjects the culture concept to critical scrutiny, see Victoria E. Bonnell and Lynn Hunt, eds., *Beyond the Cultural Turn* (Berkeley: University of California Press, 1999). The goal of these essays seems to be to clarify and improve the culture concept, rather than to offer particularly radical critiques of its application.

19 Hans Joas, *Do We Need Religion?* (Boulder: Paradigm, 2008).

religion is the precondition for apostasy, not its opposite. Two of the essays in this volume investigate what it means for someone who explicitly disavows traditional religion to continue to pursue questions rooted in a religious frame of reference. There is also the inherent, ever-present possibility of failure. According to a view of religion as culture, the hallmark effects of religion—consolation, conviction, belief, etc.—are said to have their cause in the way religion provides believers with absolute and authoritative solutions. But sometimes, the process fails. Sometimes, the rites, rituals, and all manner of intellectual and spiritual exercises fail to transform an individual into a believer or, at least, into a believer of the right kind. Sometimes, self-transcendence leads to different or unforeseen outcomes, or to none at all.[20] Seen in this way, perhaps the failure of religion is much broader and more integral to religion than we generally suppose. If history shows anything, it is that the failure of meaning and belief is just as much to be expected as robustly "religious" avowals of unquestioning faith. On this view, religion does not just diminish the threat of chaos and meaninglessness, it conduces to it.[21]

Precisely because it is said to be about "ultimate concerns," religion is often cast in such a way that competing commitments appear to present a singular choice based on a mutually exclusive and exhaustive dichotomy, like religion or science, or the almost monolithic opposition faith or reason (and its many attendant pairings, "religious/secular," "medieval/modern," etc.). I am not denying that these pairings are, and can be, experienced as deeply felt dichotomies, especially when they form structuring elements of a personal crisis. At the same time, it is to understand just how and why these terms serve as such compelling emotional antipodes, that I suggest we try to understand better how the great variety of religious experience *includes* what is quickly dismissed under headings like apostasy, heresy, and

20 Menocchio, the sixteenth-century miller that is the subject of Ginzburg's wonderful history, is nothing if not unpredictable in his account of the religious currents that went into making up his particular religious worldview. See Carlo Ginzburg, *The Cheese and the Worms. The Cosmos of a Sixteenth-Century Miller*, trans. John and Anne Tedeschi (Baltimore: Johns Hopkins UP, 1980).

21 For more on the ways that ancient religions established order out of what they perceived as the welter of chaos, see Mircea Eliade, *The Sacred and the Profane* (New York: Harcourt, 1959).

deconversion.[22] For what is rarely, if ever, asked is how what is said to be mutually incompatible can serve as answers to the same questions. How do these particular options "fit" the same terrain? Do they do so without remainder? Does the claim to occupy the same cognitive terrain betoken an instance of questions lost and forgotten to the lifeworld, as Husserl showed? Part of the answer might well involve seeing ambivalence as constitutive of belief rather than its antithesis. To see ambivalence at play in religion does not invalidate the strength of convictions. On the contrary, it helps us take account of how people very often hold multiple and even conflicting commitments at the same time, and it suggests that this might be as productive a state of affairs as it is unsettling. Mild, serious, or even crisis-causing, ambivalence undercuts the assumption that religion is immune to self-doubt, and therefore to change and even self-transformation. Instead of thwarting meaning, ambivalence may be what enables one to hold open multiple and competing possibilities at the same time, either in the search for closure or as part of the search for new and fruitful alternatives. While it is certainly true that religion does much to fix the human person in a meaningful world, it is equally true that religion does much to frustrate meaning by promoting unsettling and even subversive kinds of self-reflection. Just as every revolution is fundamentally a civil war—until it succeeds—religious revivals (even of the traditionalist sort) always contain within them potent criticisms of the status quo. Though religious authorities might be inclined to downplay this fact, historians are not obligated to do the same. And I'm not suggesting that they do so, knowingly. But the overwhelming tendency, it seems to me, has been to continue to accept somewhat uncritically the terms we have inherited from thousands of years of (largely Christian) history. And, simply put, that has led us to miss entirely the creative thrust of so much "tradition" and "fundamentalism," and to reduce all revivals to reactions, as though this was the antithesis of revolution rather than an integral part of it.

The essays in this collection do not address the issue of religious experience

22 Ann Taves does a good job of sketching the problems associated with scholars using first-order terms in their study of religion in Ann Taves, *Religious Experience Reconsidered: A Building Block Approach to the Study of Religion* (Princeton N.J.: Princeton UP, 2009), 25.

directly. Instead, they seek to deepen our knowledge of public religion by analyzing a set of episodes involving the intersection of religion with politics and culture in the long nineteenth century. They are case studies whose goal is to show how a range of ideas and behaviors that secularization would see consigned to the past are fully consonant with modernity, fully consonant with modern modes of public self-assertion, and more than capable of innovating on their own terms. In them, I try and sharpen our sense for how religious actors adapted to the demands of modernity by molding themselves—often in ways both unconscious and unintentional—to the circumstances and patterns cast by opponents. There exists a deep structural affinity between religious actors and their critics, one borne of competition, that involves innovative and public modes of self-assertion that cannot be reduced to a static understanding of culture as tradition, an affinity that I have elected to call "devotional activism." Though not the most elegant of phrases, devotional activism aims at illuminating a range of pragmatic responses to challenges that is only dimly suggested by the term "adaptation," given how the latter always puts religious actors in the position of playing catch-up. But to see these, one must look beyond the typical, and frankly hackneyed, application of "conservative," "traditional," and "reactionary" to the manifold ways that religious self-understanding is deployed against the rising tide of distinctly modern accounts of what religion is and should be. Though rejoinders to these latter were frequently framed as appeals to traditions, they were of necessity much more, since they involved reworking "tradition" to serve as compelling alternatives and, perhaps more importantly, since they enjoined their defenders to frame their positions in ways at least consonant with the evaluative criteria of their opponents.[23] Viewed as devotional activism, the fight for religion in the nineteenth century was many and varied.

There is a rich and important literature in the field of religious studies that shows how the category "religion" has deep roots in Western, Christian, and more specifically Protestant presuppositions, and how it has been used to discriminate unfairly against a whole range of faith traditions.[24] There

---

23 Even when rejecting such criteria, interlocutors in a debate must imagine how they will be understood by each other, and this exerts pressure (however subtle) on the terms used to define and make sense of a situation.

24 Brent Nongbri, *Before Religion*, op. cit.

are good reasons therefore to use the term with great care, and to resist applying it broadly. At the same time, there is no denying how the term is a mainstay of political punditry and everyday discourse, used in schools and coffee shops, to refer to what people say and do in the name of God(s) and more or less formal religious communities. It has, for better or worse, become entrenched as a way of speaking and thinking, and so if I echo this uncritical use of the term in what follows it is not out of indifference but rather because it seems to me that we can neither dispense with the term, nor simply ignore how it is used. Any account of public religion must necessarily involve itself in a fraught attempt at distinguishing what is and is not workable in common-sense notions about religion, however messy the results might be.

The chapters that follow were all written as essays. They pursue no systematic goal, aside from the themes outlined above, and can be read in any order. Chapter one addresses more fully my concern for the prevalent assumption that to be religious is to be certain, and proposes some possibilities for rethinking this assumption. In chapter two, I address the growing popularity of political theology as a rubric for thinking differently about religion in the modern world, and analyze how Carl Schmitt appealed to nineteenth-century Catholicism as a significant touchstone for articulating his conception of political theology. Chapter three tells the story of a polemic between French and German Catholics that erupted during the First World War. By looking at the specific ways French and German Catholics accused each other of a reversion to barbarism, the paper shows how such accusations served each side as a strategic bid for their domestic rehabilitation. Chapter four revisits the much vaunted "war" between science and religion. It explores how Andrew Dickson White, noted historian of the conflict, was an unorthodox—but no less religious—innovator. In the final chapter, I show how Franz Brentano's views on philosophy and religion combined to shape his views on progress, and how he drew on his experience with assimilated Viennese Jews to formulate a conception of a "New Christianity." Together, these essays are suggestive of an approach to religion in history that might broadly be considered post-secular, in the sense that it rejects the normative presumptions of a definite arc to modern history that prefigures where religion should and will "end up." At the same time, I do not place much stock in "post" secular to the extent that, like "post" modern, it is a rubric that deploys an epochal consciousness that it claims to reject. In that sense, I would like to believe that the essays here pursue a slightly more radical critique of historical consciousness, an issue to which I return in the epilogue.

CHAPTER ONE
RELIGION, UNCERTAINTY,
AND THE LIMITS OF CULTURE

"Religion and culture" is a conjunction whose significance seems to go without saying. Indeed, what could be more obvious than the fact that religion and culture shape each other in important ways, and that one of the urgent tasks confronting us today is to understand better the reciprocal influence between the great variety of religions and cultures in our world? And yet, as deeply interwoven as they no doubt are, religion and culture are not the same thing. This point needs to be stressed, for it has become somewhat commonplace today to think about religion in the same way that we think about culture. Reinforced by the ever-expanding discussion surrounding globalization and multiculturalism, this view takes for granted that culture is the primary matrix of human experience, and that religion is the crucible of a culture's values. As the foundation for thought and action, religion is what orients people in our increasingly complex world. A good example of this approach is the rationale offered for the *Faith and Globalisation Initiative*. Launched in 2008, under the auspices of Tony Blair's "Faith Foundation," the *Initiative* aimed to promote research and education on religion at major universities throughout the world.[1]

> Wherever you look today, religion matters. Faith motivates. Understanding faith, its adherents, its trends, its structures, can be as important as understanding a nation's GDP, its business, its resources. Religious awareness is as important as gender or race awareness. For politicians, business people, or ordinary interested

---

1   Though I confine myself in this essay to discussing mainly the United States, with an occasional reference to Europe, I think that the attitude might be broadly characterized as "Western."

citizens, to know about a country's faith perspective is an essential part of comprehending it. As religiosity increases in the world, understanding religion becomes ever more crucial to peaceful co-existence.[2]

The focus here on "a country's faith perspective" is telling, for by assuming (somewhat cavalierly) that religions and nations coincide, it suggests that the real objective of interest is national culture. Religion almost always cuts across national boundaries, and there are few if any nations that do not contain religious minorities. More importantly, it frames globalization as an always potentially hostile encounter between national cultures whose resolution depends on understanding religion. The website thus goes on to say: "As religiosity increases in the world, understanding religion becomes ever more crucial to peaceful co-existence.… The speed of change is one of the leading characteristics of today's world. Movements, swirls of opinion, waves of change arise, build momentum and come crashing down against our preconceived positions or notions with bewildering velocity."[3] To allay the disorienting effects of global confusion, at least according to the *Faith and Globalisation Initiative*, requires a deeper grasp of the religious roots of how others think and live.

This is not the only view of course, but it is a popular one, and it is increasingly taking on the hue of common sense. In this essay, I want to challenge the tendency to view religion as the structuring principle of culture by interrogating the assumption that religion provides a stable foundation for values because it is based on certain knowledge.[4] Far from always self-conscious, this tendency consists in treating religion as a way of knowing something about oneself in relation to society, the state etc., where this knowledge is presented as consisting in absolute claims about a transcendent

2   Accessed January 7, 2009 at: www.fgi-tbff.org/about/why-is-fgi-important.
3   Ibid.
4   In what follows I refer to "certain" in its everyday, colloquial sense of a person who gives his or her full, conscious assent to ideas or propositions considered beyond serious doubt. In the same way, I echo the colloquial use of "religion" throughout this essay to denote the beliefs and activities of those who act in the name of their God(s) and Church(es), since it is that usage that serves as the substantive correlate of "culture."

order. While most commentators acknowledge that religion is a multi-faceted phenomenon that involves practice as well as ideas, there nevertheless prevails a decidedly strong assumption among media pundits, politicians, educated elites, and even some scholars that the core of being religious is being certain about what is real and permanent versus illusory and passing. This certainty then guides decision-making in conscious, but more often unconscious, ways. What is particularly striking is how this assumption is shared by both supporters and critics of religion. In the United States, as James Davison Hunter has shown, there is no shortage of Christians who believe that what is at stake in the so-called culture wars is a battle over values. And these Christians take as their starting assumption that "the reason Christians do not have more influence in shaping culture is that Christians are just not trying hard enough, acting decisively enough, or believing strongly or Christianly enough."[5] Though Hunter questions whether culture can be reduced to values alone, he helps us see how those leading the fight are certain they will win, not only because they are on the side of right, but because their conviction and commitment guarantees it. In this context, ambivalence or ambiguity are proof positive of the insidious and corrosive effects of secular doubt. It is thus not surprising that, on the other side of the culture wars, atheists are especially quick to point to the danger of a "believer [who] is possessed of murderous certainty."[6] In his account of the "new atheists," Phil Ryan points to an underlying symmetry structuring the debate: "The New Atheist asserts that when believers get serious, they get ugly. The defender asserts that when atheists get serious, they get ugly.... Each side can allow that there are decent members of the opposing camp, but then claim that the decent types are not fully serious, not true to their fundamental world view."[7] This dynamic has only grown stronger in the wake of the *Charlie Hebdo* murders and similar instances of violence, and talk show host Bill Maher's denunciations of Islam as "like the Mafia" are emblematic of the trend.

5   Hunter, *To Change the World: The Irony, Tragedy and Possibility of Christianity in the Late Modern World* (New York: Oxford University Press, 2010), 22.
6   Phil Ryan, *After the New Atheist Debate* (Toronto: University of Toronto Press, 2014), 65.
7   Ibid.

But the salient point is that, on all sides, being religious is presented as a state of pure conviction, a certainty about the truth, whose stakes involve nothing short of life and death.

The notion that religion functions chiefly as a generative source of meaning encourages a view of religious people as fundamentally certain about themselves and their faith. This essay explores how justified we are in this assumption. By evaluating a sample of some recent discourse about religion located at the intersection between scholarship, politics, and media punditry, it tries to illuminate how this assumption informs different positions in this discourse. It also suggests ways in which doubt and uncertainty, fear and trembling, ambivalence and even indifference might be better factored into the religious equation. I do not deny that there are many who are certain in their beliefs, and who act on those beliefs without a second thought. But I am skeptical that these people and their particular kind of experience should be the model for understanding the multiple and complex dimensions of religion. The essay argues that we must find room for these facets of experience in how we understand religion, or risk misunderstanding the ways that religion does—as well as does not—shape culture.

Religion as Culture

There is no room here to provide a detailed overview of the transition to "culture" as a research paradigm in the social sciences and humanities. To be sure, any such history would have to address structural and later cultural anthropology, semiotics, and a range of lesser-known efforts in phenomenology, lifeworld sociology, and philosophical anthropology. One would also have to look at the emergence of a distinct "Western" Marxist critique of culture, and its influence in the rise of cultural studies. What is essential, however, is the idea that human life is symbolic through and through. To live and operate in the world—to have a "world" at all—means to inhabit a dense network of symbols that both enable and constrain how one "sees" and understands things. Above all else, it is symbolic networks that govern the range of possible courses of action one might take and the choices one makes. In what might arguably be taken as the paradigmatic formulation of culture, Clifford Geertz defines culture as "an historically transmitted pattern of meanings embodied in symbols, a system of inherited conceptions expressed in symbolic forms by means of which men communicate, perpetuate, and develop their knowledge and attitude about and towards life."[8] Culture is thus less a fixed body of folk tales, art, literature, or music than a set of tacit rules for producing what is accepted as intelligible by members of the same culture. These rules can and do change, but are not easily dispensed with, since they form the conditions for any possible understanding of what it means to live in a given place and time. In contrast with the objectivizing imperative of so much older social science, whose mandate was to systematically analyze, measure, define, categorize, and catalogue the range of social practice, "culture" offers ways of seeing individuals and groups as decidedly active participants in their own—near constant—self-definition and self-fashioning. It also offers new and interesting ways to understand change; for if culture constrains how members express themselves, it also provides important avenues for breaking the rules in ways that themselves have symbolic meaning. To break a taboo in the right way is to exploit the subversive potential of a given culture, and to illuminate alternative ways of doing things. Having grasped this, many scholars now devote great energy to documenting the subversive strategies of subaltern groups and identifying the often hidden forms of agency through which individuals take some measure of control—however limited—over their own lives, even when subject to the rules of larger symbolic networks.[9] To think about religion along these lines provides a powerful explanatory matrix for showing how religious ideas and actions are interwoven with a larger and powerful symbolic order. And it offers a way to see how religion can be internally contested by practitioners whose lack of formal power doesn't necessarily leave them without resources for articulating alternatives to what religious leaders say is the nature of the faith.[10] This is not to deny the ways that religions can and do enforce orthodoxy. But seen from the point of view of culture, the power of

8   Clifford Geertz, "Religion as a Cultural System," in *The Interpretation of Cultures* (New York: Basic Books, 1973), 89.

9   Michel de Certeau, *The Practice of Everyday Life* (Los Angeles: UC Press, 1984).

10   Dipesh Chakrabarty, *Provincializing Europe: Postcolonial Thought and Historical Difference* (Princeton: Princeton University Press, 2000).

religion lies not so much in how its leaders enforce conformity as it does in its capacity to have members internalize these rules as their own.

The centrality of culture in the humanities and social sciences, though not unchallenged, has had a decisive influence on the study of religion.[11] In their summary of "the emerging strong program in the sociology of religion," David Smilde and Matthew May surveyed 587 articles in three general sociology journals between 1978 and 2007. They found that, in addition to an overall rise in the number of articles addressing religion, there was a shift in the way it was perceived. In contrast to social scientific literature from the 1960s and early 70s, when religion was evaluated in light of more basic social processes, religion is now increasingly featured as the primary independent variable. They conclude that the driving force behind this shift is the tendency to consider religion primarily as a phenomenon of culture: "The most basic building block of any strong program is the idea that culture is an autonomous phenomenon that is not reducible to social circumstances. The usual way of arguing for the autonomy of culture is by maintaining that it consists of a system of symbols that are substantially arbitrary."[12] Because these symbols are arbitrary, it is thus their specific way of interacting that endows them with meaning, and "[t]his internal determination of meaning is what then gives culture the power to constitute social reality rather than vice versa." When applied to religion, "religion becomes an autonomous, irreducible phenomenon that can thus function as an independent variable," and this autonomy, in turn, helps explain just how religion serves as the foundation for meaning in a culture more generally.

For Smilde and May, definite normative assumptions underwrite this view of the autonomy of religion and culture. In their view, treating culture as an autonomous, independent variable involves a deeply political commitment to the "key element of human dignity and freedom."[13] Viewing

11 For important and substantive critiques of the hegemony of culture as a paradigm in history, see Victoria E. Bonnell and Lynn Hunt, eds., *Beyond the Cultural Turn* (Berkeley: University of California, 1999).

12 David Smilde and Matthew May, *The Emerging Strong Program in the Sociology of Religion: A Critical Engagement* (New York: Social Science Research Council Working Papers), 4.

13 Ibid., 5.

culture as irreducible helps establish the individual as the primary agent who shapes the social world and is responsible for it, and who is thus not simply the product of larger social forces. At the same time, however, the presumed universality of this agent, rather than effacing real social differences attached to all subjects, normalizes assumptions about the masculine, logocentric—and ultimately Western—ideals of autonomous action. Smilde and May also point out that the imbrication of freedom and dignity with cultural autonomy in this way encourages a degree of "pro-religiousness" to the degree that religion is taken to promote the free, autonomous individual. It furthermore leads to seeing religion a certain way: "When the concept of religion as a deeply-held, autonomous set of beliefs becomes the baseline for conceptualizing religion, religious practices that do not fit this model are often portrayed as insincere, vacillating, superficial, or impermanent."[14] To give an example, one sees this kind of preference at work in the U.S. Department of State annual International Report on Religious Freedom, which is based almost exclusively on the degree to which states acknowledge the individual right to religious freedom, and virtually ignores other modes of religious being.[15] One sees a similar focus on the individual in the Council of Europe's 2008 *Recommendation* addressing "dimensions of religious and non-religious convictions within intercultural education."[16] As Hent de Vries points out, to the extent that the document opposes unthinking "cult" to a more reflective "culture," "what is distinguished and … separated here is a certain diffuse and uncritical '*appartenance*' or 'belonging,' on the one hand, and an '*autoconstitution*' or 'self-constitution' on the other."[17]

Clifford Geertz's essay "Religion as a Cultural System" has been enormously influential in shaping how many scholars view the close connection between culture and religion.[18] One might even say that it has been more

---

14 Ibid.

15 Accessed January 7, 2009 at: http://www.state.gov/j/drl/irf/.

16 *Dimensions of Religions and Non-Religious Convictions within Intercultural Education* (Strasbourg: Council of Europe Publishing, 2009).

17 Hent de Vries, "A Religious Canon for Europe? Policy, Education, and the Postsecular Challenge," in *Social Research* 80: 1 (Spring 2013): 211.

18 William H. Sewell, "Geertz, Cultural Systems, and History: From Synchrony to Transformation," in *Representations* 59 (Summer 1997): 35–55.

influential outside of anthropology than inside the discipline.[19] In it, Geertz defines religion as "a system of symbols which acts to establish powerful, pervasive and long-lasting moods and motivations in men by formulating conceptions of a general order of existence and clothing these conceptions with such an aura of factuality that the moods and motivations seem uniquely realistic."[20] Religions are powerful because they provide an effective means of reconciling people to the "inescapability of ignorance, pain and injustice" in the world. Religious rituals are especially important, because they reassure believers that the transcendent order guaranteed by religion is, in fact, capable of exerting real force in the world. Rituals offer participants an immediate experience of the authority of the order they ultimately find so reassuring: "Having ritually 'leapt' … into the framework of meaning which religious conceptions define, and the ritual ended, returned again to the common-sense world, a man is—unless, as sometimes happens, the experience fails to register—changed. And as he is changed, so also is the common-sense world, for it is now seen as but the partial form of a wider reality which corrects and completes it."[21] On this view, the authority of religion is internalized as the certainty that begets a life-changing experience. Anything short of this is, according to Geertz, the failure of religion.

There are many things to consider when assessing the current preference for seeing religion as essentially cultural, and Geertz's essay comprises only one of those factors. But what cannot be denied is how influential this way of looking at things has become, even in the face of criticism. One of Geertz's most incisive critics has been Talal Asad, who calls "Geertz's treatment of religious belief … a modern, privatized Christian one … to the extent that it emphasizes the priority of belief as a state of mind."[22] He

19 Geertz exerted enormous influence among American academics in large part given his position as founding director of the social sciences section of the Institute for Advanced Study. For more on his influence among historians, see Natalie Zemon Davis, "Remembering Clifford Geertz," in *History Workshop Journal* 65 (Spring 2008): 188–94.

20 Geertz, "Religion as a Cultural System," 90.

21 Ibid., 122.

22 Talal Asad, "Anthropological Conceptions of Religion: Reflections on Geertz," in *Man* 18 (1983), p. 247. Some have argued that Geertz is more sophisticated than Asad allows. In his defense of Geertz, for example, Kevin Schilbrack

challenges the way Geertz universalizes a conception of religion based on rationalist assumptions, and argues that Geertz's claim that religion helps people live with "ignorance, pain, and injustice" hardly seems to differentiate religion from any philosophical or ethical system, or address the many facets of real, historical religions.[23] By treating symbols primarily as tools of understanding, Geertz interprets religion as theory, and pays short shrift to how religion comprises historically situated systems of authority for distributing real power in concrete situations. Of course, religious studies scholars have long been mindful of reducing religion to belief, and there is a solid body of literature that exposes the Western, and ultimately Christian, underpinning of that tendency.[24] Asad's critique is not so different from what Robert Bellah, writing in the 1960s, called the "objectivist fallacy." For Bellah, intellectuals primarily concerned with how religion maintained social order "assimilated revelation to an objectivist cognitive framework as though what was revealed were 'higher' cognitive truths rather than the direct confrontation with the divine that the Bible is concerned with."[25] This perpetuated "a sophisticated error in understanding the religious life of the ordinary man" as "primarily a matter of objectivist belief."[26] The problem with eliding religion and "faith" or "belief," is that it carries with it normative expectations for how religious people should be able to frame their experience, and can thus be used as a way of discriminating between "true" religion and various inferior varieties.[27] Unfortunately, this criticism remains

points out that Geertz does not even use the word "belief" in his essay, and argues that Geertz's work is too deeply influenced by Wittgenstein's view on the public character of language to be characterized as preoccupied with private meaning. See K. Schilbrack, "Religion, Models Of, and Reality: Are We Through with Geertz?" in *Journal of the American Academy of Religion* 73 no. 2 (2005): 429–52.

23 Asad, "The Construction of Religion as an Anthropological Category," op. cit.

24 Catherine M. Bell, "Paradigms Behind (and Before) the Study of Religion," in *History and Theory* 45:4 (2006): 27–46.

25 Bellah, "Religion and Belief," in *Beyond Belief: Essays on Religion in a Post-Traditionalist World* (Los Angeles: University of California Press, 1991), 221.

26 Ibid., 220.

27 Wilfred Cantwell Smith, *The Meaning and End of Religion* (Minneapolis: Fortress Press, 1991).

largely confined to scholars working in the field of religious studies. Outside the field, simple notions of "faith" and "belief" continue to serve as part of the ineluctable *lingua franca* for talking about religion. And these, in turn, reinforce common-sense ideas about how religion consists in absolute convictions that drive motives about right action in the world.

Taking stock of the ways that religion is conceived as culture is important given how more and more people see religion as the master key to unlocking the sources of global order and disorder. This trend is especially evident in the growing prevalence in the media and politics of what Mahmood Mamdani calls "culture talk." "Culture talk assumes that every culture has a tangible essence that defines it, and then explains politics as a consequence of that essence."[28] Culture talk has emerged in recent decades as an especially potent way of discussing Islam, but is no less active in discussion of Christian and other fundamentalisms. It is often validated by citing the work of scholars like Bernard Lewis and Samuel Huntington, who offer geopolitical narratives of the clash of civilizations that reaffirm the defining role of religion in history.[29] And it is reinforced by diffuse but nevertheless powerful presuppositions underwriting how most people think about the course of modern history itself. To be modern, after all, is to be among the peoples who self-consciously create culture, and who are thus the authors of their own progress. Culture talk presents Muslims and a range of religious and civilizational "others" as either pre-modern or anti-modern. In either case, "history seems to have petrified into a lifeless custom," and culture "stands for habit, for some kind of instinctive activity with rules that are inscribed in early founding texts, usually religious, and mummified in early artifacts.[30]

Culture talk is especially influential among those who claim that religion is inherently violent because it proffers absolute claims. On this view, religion establishes incontestable truths for believers, and so legitimizes violence as an appropriate tool to transform the world in the name of what is known to be good, right, and true. The problem with this view, of course, is that ideological absolutism is not exclusive to religion. As William Cavanaugh points

---

28 Mamdani, *Good Muslim, Bad Muslim*, op. cit., 17.
29 Samuel Huntington, *The Clash of Civilizations and the Remaking of World Order* (New York: Simon & Schuster, 2011).
30 Mamdani, *Good Muslim, Bad Muslim*, op. cit., 18.

out, the number of Americans "willing to kill for their country" is probably far greater than the number of Americans who would "identify themselves as willing to kill for their Christian faith."[31] This raises important questions for those who hold that religion "has a much greater tendency toward fanaticism because the object of its truth claims is absolute in ways that secular claims are not." For Cavanaugh, the claim that religion breeds violence is thus really part of a strategy for legitimizing secular violence. Since the religious violence frequently under discussion today is almost exclusively non-Western, the goal is really to establish a dichotomy between a rational, secular, moderate West and those still beholden to absolutist, religious impulses. Exponents of this view "attribute Muslims' animosity toward the West to their inability to learn the lessons of history and remove the baneful influence of religion from politics." But, as Cavanaugh points out, this way of thinking depends on a "blind spot regarding our own history of violence," a violence that is allegedly only ever used reluctantly, in the name of self-defense or lofty and selfless goals such as the defense of international law.[32] The result is an image of the West as "a monolithic reality representing modernity, which necessarily includes secularity and rationality," and an image of the Muslim world as "an equally monolithic reality which is ancient, that is, lagging behind modernity, because of its essentially religious and irrational character."[33] Viewed in this way, Western violence is justified because it liberates others from being stuck in a backwards and regressive culture.[34]

When Religion Fails

Treating religion as culture depends on a notion of the human person as a meaning-making machine, ceaselessly navigating and deploying dense

31 William T. Cavanaugh, "Does Religion Cause Violence?" in *Harvard Divinity Bulletin* (Spring/Summer 2007): 6.

32 Ibid., 7–8.

33 Ibid., 9.

34 I certainly do not mean to ignore those who cite their religious certainties as grounds for violence. That would be irresponsible in the extreme. But religion is not reducible to the violence carried out in its name, and there is a distinct circularity in so many accounts that seek to explain religious violence by claiming that religion is inherently violent.

symbolic networks that are assumed to be transparent to those embedded in them.[35] This is never explicitly stated. But to the extent that culture is construed as symbols—as so much text to be read—then its intelligibility remains the implicit goal of cultural analysis. This is underscored by the fact that the failure of meaning, while always acknowledged as a possibility, is largely treated as peripheral. For Geertz, the failure of meaning is precisely what religion ensures against by serving as a bulwark against the "tumult of events which lack not just interpretations but interpretability."[36] The failure of meaning only becomes central when it is so widespread as to initiate a meltdown. It is not, in principle, part of the system itself. Above all, religion does not itself encourage vacillation, much less serve as a source of welcome, compelling, or even productive confusion. Indeed, religion is taken as the paradigmatic case of certainty, precisely because it resolves existential difficulties and provides a blueprint for action. It provides believers with desperately needed answers in the face of a threatening and complex world. And this is not just Geertz's view. In his account of the ways humanity seeks to escape the "terror of history," Teofilo Ruiz writes:

> Religion or religious experiences, in its (or their) many different variations means essentially the way in which one (or the many) places oneself in the hands of god (or the gods). Religion posits the terrors besetting one's own personal life and the weight of collective history as part of a divine plan and as the sum total of inscrutable but always wise actions of an all-powerful, all-knowing deity (or deities). The religious man or woman will often find great solace in belief. Though god's (or the gods') actions often seem inexplicable and cruel, there is always the reassuring belief that the deity knows why such things need to happen. There is, after all, a higher purpose. In the end, all events, awful and good, form part of an over-arching sacred project in which we all play a part.[37]

35 For a good account of the uncertainty constitutive of religious language, see Mark Schaefer, *The Certainty of Uncertainty: The Way of Inescapable Doubt and Its Virtue*, op. cit.
36 Geertz, "Religion as a Cultural System," op. cit., 100.
37 Ruiz, *The Terror of History* (Princeton: Princeton University Press, 2011), 18.

It is remarkable how broadly both proponents and opponents of religion share this view, namely, that religion supplies people with answers, and that the ultimate impulse driving people towards religion is a need for certainty in the face of meaninglessness. Iconic figures such as the monk, the activist, the convert, the missionary, the pilgrim, the hermit, the martyr, the saint virtually define what it means to be sure, so sure that one pursues a goal at all costs. This, in spite of the fact that the real lives of so many people—religious *virtuosi* included—often involve sustained and serious doubt. Though it is not something I can pursue here, one might wonder whether and to what extent these figures serve as a pantheon for managing uncertainty. How are such figures deployed throughout history as leading characters in a narrative that features doubt and crisis, but only as a prelude to arriving at a new level of religious awareness and devotion? From this perspective, one might read Augustine's *Confessions* as paradigmatic of a whole genre of writing that treats crisis as a kind of spiritual deficit brought on by a surfeit of intellect whose resolution is nevertheless a new level of certainty. After all, Augustine "is led ... to prefer the Catholic doctrine" because it is "more unassuming and honest, in that she required to be believed things not demonstrated ... whereas among the Manichees our credulity was mocked by a promise of certain knowledge, and then so many most fabulous and absurd things were imposed to be believed because they could not be demonstrated."[38]

Contemporary discussions depend heavily on the presumption that religion is (and must be) a pursuit of absolute meaning; that religious experience doesn't consist, perhaps, to some very great extent, in having meaning thwarted, in having questions not answered, in being unsettled rather than reassured. What about those instances when people are not certain? What about those instances when they know little, or are incorrect, even about their own faith traditions? In 2010, results from the Pew "U.S. Religious

---

38 Augustine, *The Confessions of Saint Augustine*, trans. Edward B. Pusey (Ashland, 2007), 83. In his account of the Victorian "crisis of faith," Christopher Lane explores how it "generated a far more serious engagement with all facets of religious belief and doubt," and concludes that as a result "Victorians came to view doubt as inseparable from belief." See Christopher Lane, *The Age of Doubt: Tracing the Roots of Our Religious Uncertainty* (New Haven: Yale UP, 2011), 4.

Knowledge Survey" suggested that Americans know surprisingly little about religion. Not unexpectedly, perhaps, knowledge of world religions was especially poor. Only about half of those surveyed knew that the Koran was the Islamic holy book. Less than half knew that the Dalai Lama is Buddhist. And only 27% of those surveyed knew that Indonesia is mostly Muslim. Knowledge of Christianity was better, but even here only about half of respondents knew that the "Golden Rule" was not one of the ten commandments. Slightly less than half knew that Martin Luther inspired the Reformation, and only 11% knew that Jonathan Edwards participated in the First Great Awakening. But even more startling, perhaps, was the lack of knowledge about key Christian doctrines. Only slightly more than half of Catholics knew that the bread and wine do more than symbolize the body and blood of Christ, and only 16% of respondents knew that Protestants (and not Catholics) taught the doctrine of salvation by faith alone.

One way to read the results, of course, is to conclude that Americans know much less about religion than perhaps they ought to, given the relatively high levels of religious membership in the United States.[39] Another possibility, however, is to ask whether there really are specific things that religious people ought to know, and that by not knowing them, they therefore compromise their religious authenticity. Would better scores really tell us something significant about what religion means to people? The very preference for asking about people like Martin Luther and Jonathan Edwards betrays a kind of canonical approach that hardly gets at the way religion is lived in everyday life. To understand religion, should we focus on

---

39 Many assume that the erosion of religious knowledge in the U.S. is the direct result of a secularist agenda. Stephen Prothero argues that the real cause lies in the historical decision to tone down religious education that stressed doctrinal and other differences in order to provide a common Protestant basis for hostility to what were considered the "real" enemies—namely, Catholics and Jews. This common Protestant identity was further reinforced throughout the century as Protestants sought common ground when working together on a range of issues from abolition to temperance to civil rights. In all of these cases, American Protestants downplayed differences that otherwise might have prevented them from banding together as effectively as they did. Stephen R. Prothero, *Religious Literacy: What Every American Needs to Know—and Doesn't*, first edition (San Francisco: Harper Collins, 2007).

what people don't know? Or is it perhaps better to try and understand what they do know, and how their knowledge and ignorance work together to sustain religious life day in and day out? Is it really that surprising that just under half of the Catholics polled failed to identify the doctrine of transubstantiation? Isn't the more interesting question just how these Catholics maintain their Catholic identity in the face of what clearly is a doctrinal blind spot? Couldn't one speculate that the manifest difficulty of accepting this particular doctrine, in a scientific age such as ours, reflects a distinct and calculated preference for not "knowing" certain things? Isn't the real issue to find out just how the great variety of religious people participate in their religious communities: on what terms, with what hopes, desires, questions, and yes, even elisions, contradictions, and mistakes? If people lack knowledge about their own religious traditions does that mean that they are less religious? Does it mean they are insincerely religious? It does, if we take as our working hypothesis that religion consists in knowing for sure. But what if we are prepared to accept that a lack of knowledge might itself be woven into religious experience in certain ways? What if being religious means abiding faithfully with a certain amount of ignorance, and maybe even longing for it to some extent?

These are important questions if one wants to understand what actually happens in the many and varied lives of those people who call themselves religious. But to answer them requires accepting that these lives are as fraught with experiences of inconsistency, contradiction, and meaninglessness as any other; that religion doesn't immunize anyone against these very human realities. What is especially interesting in Ruiz's characterization of religion as an escape from the "terror of history" is how it fails to sufficiently appreciate what it means to gamble everything on faith. Far from simply taking the easy way out, the person who assigns responsibility for the terror of history to God—with nothing less than a promise that this will be made good in some unknown future—actually holds God responsible for things that are otherwise more easily explained away as history. Looking for the answers in history is much less risky, since historical understanding finds specific and local causes for events that hardly implicate God.[40] To be sure,

40   J. G. A. Pocock, "Historiography and Enlightenment: A View of Their History," in *Modern Intellectual History* 5 (2008): 83–96.

placing the blame for history at the feet of God might be comforting, but it might just as well place one's faith in serious jeopardy. Viewed in this way, religion might involve accepting a level of anxiety that challenges facile conclusions about how religion serves primarily as a source of comfort and certainty. At the very least, it should prompt a more critical response to those who insist that "[m]odernity ... undermine[s] the taken for granted certainties by which people lived through most of history," and therefore "religious movements that claim to give certainty have great appeal."[41] Given religion's central place among these older certainties, one must ask just why religion persists when other pre-modern certainties dissolve in the face of modernity. What particular quality does religion have that other "taken for granted" certainties do not? Could it be that it is not certainty, as such, but perhaps rather a certain rhythmic encounter between doubt and certainty that—far from being resolved by ritual or other means—is placed perpetually before the religious as a burden to shoulder or a challenge to meet? Could it be that religion offers a unique way to dwell with uncertainty?

Of course, to even contemplate looking at religion this way flies in the face of the common-sense view that holds that what makes people religious is their fidelity to ideas that are beyond doubt. According to this line of thought: *To be religious is to believe, and one must accept at least the basic tenets of the faith in a way that concedes to them some authority, even if one doesn't agree with everything. And in religions that are not based on formal doctrine, practice is the essential characteristic. To be religious is to do what is consistent with the religious community, and to do it appropriately, that is to say, in the right place, at the right time, and in the right way. One can be doubtful, but doubt constitutes a measure of the distance from being truly religious. While there is a kind of doubt that precipitates crisis and deeper religious devotion, anything else is ultimately corrosive. Religious fundamentalism, religious violence, religious bigotry illustrate only too well the immutable kernel of religion, which consists in a desire to impose a truth, held to be absolute, on the world. Those who call themselves religious moderates might reject violence and bigotry in pursuit of this goal, but they do not thereby reject an exclusive claim to truth in principle. To do so, after all, would entail not believing what one*

41 Berger, "The Desecularization of the World. A Global Overview," op. cit., 11.

claims to believe. Moderation is thus a virtue imported into religion by secular norms of tolerance. Sam Harris makes just this point very forcefully in his *The End of Faith.* For Harris, moderates are especially troublesome because they provide cover for fundamentalism to continue. Quite simply, moderates delude themselves about the true state of their beliefs, presenting their tolerance and pluralism as products of religious enlightenment rather than as the fruits of a secular culture.

> The only reason anyone is "moderate" in matters of faith these days is that he has assimilated some of the fruits of the last two thousand years of human thought (democratic politics, scientific advancement on every front, concern for human rights, an end to cultural and geographic isolation, etc.). The doors leading out of scriptural literalism do not open from the *inside.* The moderation we see among non-fundamentalists is not some sign that faith itself has evolved; it is, rather, the product of the many hammer blows of modernity that have exposed certain tenets of faith to doubt. Not the least among these developments has been the emergence of our tendency to value evidence and to be convinced by a proposition to the degree that there is evidence for it. Even most fundamentalists live by the lights of reason in this regard; it is just that their minds seem to have been partitioned to accommodate the profligate truth claims of their faith.[42]

For Harris, to be religious is to believe with full confidence in the literal meaning of sacred texts and/or the pronouncements of religious authorities. The religious moderate, by contrast, really wants to be something else, but fails to take seriously how doubt is the mind's natural (and non-religious) desire to free itself from the confines of ignorance.

In their important book, *American Grace,* Robert Putnam and David Campbell observe that the number of religious moderates is declining in the United States. Drawing from an analysis of data from the *Faith Matters*

---

42 Sam Harris, *The End of Faith: Religion, Terror, and the Future of Reason* (New York: W.W. Norton & Co., 2005), 18–19.

688888888888888

Surveys, administered to thousands of respondents in 2006 and 2007, they argue that American society is becoming increasingly polarized on the subject of religion. This is particularly interesting, given the historical fluidity of religion in American society, and the fact that people are much more likely to change religious affiliation than in almost any other society. Historically, the United States has sustained a "thriving religious ecosystem" in which "[r]eligions compete, adapt, and evolve as individual Americans freely move from one congregation to another, and even from one religion to another."[43] But in the early twenty-first century, this ecosystem seems to be eroding. An intense polarization surrounds religion today. In contrast with fifty years ago when what mattered was if you were a Catholic, Jew, or Protestant—and more specifically whether you were Irish, German, or Polish Catholic, a Methodist, Baptist, or Presbyterian—what matters now is whether one is religious or not. This polarization is shrinking the ranks of religious moderates, as people of faith square off against what they perceive to be an increasingly determined secularist critique. And here it is worth speculating whether one relevant factor driving this process might be that the emerging standard of certainty in the public discourse about religion is driving moderates to be more committed than they otherwise might be.[44]

There is no room in this essay to go into the larger and vexed issue of how reason and religion have come to be seen, by some, as opposed. But one thing that any future discussion will have to address is the puzzling way that Harris, and others like him, ascribe a strange mix of reasonableness and gullibility to those allegedly ensnared by religion's promise of certainty in an uncertain world. Why does Harris believe that the same person who so easily succumbs to the lure of faith can be awakened by the "many hammer blows of modernity that have exposed certain tenets of faith to doubt?" This seems a strange conclusion, at best, given his derisive treatment of religious believers as, basically, stupid. Harris offers two answers, neither of which is satisfactory. On the one hand, he argues that religion is a relic of

43 Ibid., 4.
44 Robert Putnam, David Campbell, and Shaylyn Romney Garrett, *American Grace: How Religion Divides and Unites Us* (New York: Simon & Schuster, 2010.)

humanity's ancient past that, over time, has been supplanted by the "tendency to value evidence" and other mental aptitudes absent in the past. But one has to wonder: if what is requisite to making good judgments about modernity and its supposed advantages are precisely those self-same mental aptitudes, then how does one suddenly come into possession of them (since the religious person, is by definition, without them)? On the other hand, he argues that people persist in being religious by partitioning their minds in such a way that truth and error are unable to mutually interrogate each other. But here too, one has to wonder: if one recognizes the validity of the truth enough to see it as a threat to belief—enough to shut it out—then the mind is not truly partitioned. On the contrary, what this suggests is that such people ultimately take on a burden of cognitive dissonance; that they live with a kind of ambivalence that hardly squares with benign reassurances that one's faith is simply "right."

Dynamic Religion/Devotional Activism

Too often, religion and culture are elided in ways that make it hard to account for how religious people actually live, with all the challenges, compromises and contradictions this entails. To remedy this state of affairs will require a better grasp of the historical pressures that shape the category "religion" and its attendant meanings, and a better grasp of the shifting historical position of different religious groups.[45] This means more than simply saying that religions change, a fact that religions themselves acknowledge but generally downplay by saying that the forces of change are extraneous to the core of ritual and belief. What is needed is a deeper appreciation of the dynamic nature of religion, and the ways that religions overwhelm their own traditions and catalyze their symbolic frameworks in innovative and creative ways. To approach religion as dynamic means looking at how

---

45 It is worth noting that the charges of anti-modernity levied against Islam today are not that much different from those levied at Catholics a century and a half ago. For a good introduction to the vexed position of Catholics vis-a-vis "modernity," see Christopher Clark and Wolfram Kaiser, eds., *Culture Wars: Secular-Catholic Conflict in Nineteenth-Century Europe* (New York: Cambridge University Press, 2003).

people strike a balance between keeping faith with one's spiritual ancestors and preparing oneself for living in the present and future with integrity. This is a point that Peter Slater makes in his *The Dynamics of Religion*, in which he argues that "[f]ailure to acknowledge the future orientation and changing patterns of religious ways of life" means that "we cannot account for the growth of traditions and convergence of conflicting points of view, except in terms of nonreligious factors. A definition which emphasizes only the sacred past ... can only describe change as decline." Without a keen sense for the internally dynamic nature of religion, "[n]ovelty in religion ... appears not as creativity but as an invitation to disaster."[46]

To approach religion as dynamic offers us new possibilities for understanding the tremendous fecundity of religion, whose history of schism, apostasy, and reformation might just as easily be written as a story of evolution, innovation, and creativity. It offers a way of conceiving of religion as something other than merely a brake on change. This is something that James Carse tries to show in his *The Religious Case Against Belief*, in which he argues that religious identity is always much bigger and more complex than the specific beliefs that are taken to define religions at any given moment. Belief defines what is right and wrong, and serves to police the boundaries of a community. But belief founders precisely to the extent that it seeks wholly to explain all things. By promulgating what is wholly certain, belief invariably defines a realm of what is outside of belief, what is false. But what is false, of course, is always in principle an alternative belief. Viewed in this way, belief and unbelief are necessarily constituted by each other.

> [B]ecause belief is always belief against, it is itself an act of unbelief. It is the active refusal to take a rival position. To believe something, one must disbelieve something. Each belief must not only have an opponent; it must have an opponent whose (dis)beliefs are a perfect match. For this reason, each is largely defined by its opposite. If beliefs die when their opposition disappears, they are obliged to mimic any changes the opposition

46 Peter Slater, *The Dynamics of Religion: Meaning and Change in Religious Traditions* (San Francisco: Harper & Row, 1978), 8.

makes of itself. Belief and unbelief are therefore locked into mutual self-creation.[47]

To ignore this dialectic between belief and unbelief is to ignore the creative, adaptive, and sometimes downright revolutionary impulses internal to religion, and how religion continually undercuts the certainty of so much that is professed as belief.[48]

To assume that to be religious means being always and everywhere certain is to assume that being religious is fully satisfying, that it brings ultimate repose instead of restlessness. It assumes that religion fills human beings to the brim, without 1) any lingering doubts about religion's adequacy in confronting a complex world, or 2) any surfeit that might just as easily spill over as a desire to change the world. For Christians, as James Davison Hunter argues, there exists a central tension surrounding the call to fulfill the absolute "spiritual and ethical requirements of the gospel" in a fallen world. To do that, means responding clearly and forcefully to whatever threatens these requirements. And yet, because it is fallen world, one cannot simply Christianize the world by acting on deep and certain convictions about God's will. Since any use of earthly "power is inherently tainted, and its use inherently compromising of the standards to which Christ beckons," it is incumbent on the Christian to realize that, "[i]n this world, the Church can never be in repose," and the best one can do is "abide in the will and purposes of God in the present world disorder with integrity."[49] This predicament helps to frame my interest in the more specific workings of devotional activism. Like all activists, the devotional activist

---

47 James P. Carse, *The Religious Case Against Belief* (New York: The Penguin Press, 2008), 42.

48 In his excellent "emotional" history of doubt, Alec Ryrie reverses typical "death of God" arguments by saying that philosophers' criticisms were not the cause, but rather the consequence, of unbelief—offering justifications for a phenomenon that had deeper roots in everyday life. His is a compelling account that verges on—but does not endorse—the position I defend here, which is that belief and unbelief are necessarily always present as options, no matter how muted one may seem at any given time. See Alec Ryrie, *Unbelievers: An Emotional History of Doubt* (Cambridge: Belknap, 2019).

49 Hunter, *To Change the World*, op. cit., 183.

understands the forces arrayed against him, and is more or less obligated to fight these in ways that frequently involve molding one's strategy after that of the opponent, willingly or unwillingly.[50] Though it is not the case that all religious protest counts as devotional activism, I do think that the following chapters illustrate compelling instances of a deep structural affinity between religious actors and their critics, one borne of competition that involves innovative and public modes of self-assertion that deepen our grasp of the dynamic character of religion.

The tremendous diversity of religious experience is often taken as the ground for rejecting a unified definition of religion. I am inclined to turn this around and say that the difficulty in conceptualizing religion suggests that this is a dimension of experience and history unlike any other. While the many and varied attempts at defining religion yield nothing like an essence or singular activity, taken together, they do suggest that religion—whatever else it is—is a long history of sometimes ecstatic and sometimes agonizing struggle over the place of humanity in the cosmos. Religion is a tradition of thinking about life and the limits of existence—in its becoming and its passing, its fullness and its emptiness, its certainties and its uncertainties—and attempting to live with integrity. When it comes to thinking about religion, therefore, what is important is not only that we recognize that the term is contested. Just as important is to ask whether this conflict over its meaning tells us something about what it means. Religion is a contested category precisely because there are multiple possibilities for what it means to be religious. Though we may not be able to define it, we know religion by its unparalleled presence in almost every historical place and time. And viewed over time, religion expresses a restlessness with every place and time, a dissatisfaction that enables the religious to cultivate a range of ideas and practices that transcend easy classification. In the end, how we understand religion will be one of the most demanding critical endeavors we have yet undertaken. Of that, we can be certain.

---

50   Of course, that is not always the case. Those who seek non-violent means to stand up to violent oppressors self-consciously reject certain tactics. But even here, it is arguable that the explicit use of nonviolence serves to highlight—and help negate—the power of violence as a means.

CHAPTER TWO
POLITICAL THEOLOGY, CARL SCHMITT,
AND NINETEENTH-CENTURY CATHOLICISM

The twenty-first century has seen a renewal of scholarly interest in religion that might seem surprising, especially given how many scholars have for so long steadfastly behaved as though religion was in progressive decline since sometime in the eighteenth century.[1] Precisely because religion has thwarted this assumption, there is today a pervasive uncertainty about just how to understand religion. What is especially perplexing, as José Casanova observes, is "the assumption of public roles by precisely those religious traditions which both theories of secularization and cyclical theories of religious revival had assumed were becoming ever more marginal and irrelevant in the modern world."[2] Rather than abandon politics for the safety of private life, in other words, religion has found creative ways to adapt and reinvigorate itself in the public sphere. Seeking to make sense of this, some have proposed that political theology is the rubric best suited to reconsidering the relationship between religion and politics. Political theology, in this context, refers to the "stories we tell ourselves about our nature as humans, our aspirations for order and justice in light of the sacred, and what, thereby, constitutes and limits legitimate rule over our collective lives."[3] Its point of departure is that it is impossible "to completely separate ... [or] to completely conflate politics and religion."[4] At this particular moment, when

1 Peter Berger, *The Desecularization of the World: Resurgent Religion and World Politics* (1999).
2 José Casanova, *Public Religions in the Modern World*, op. cit., 5.
3 Michael Jon Kessler, "Introduction: Political Theology in a Plural Context," in *Political Theology for a Plural Age*, ed., Michael Jon Kessler (Oxford University Press, 2013), 1.
4 Dimitris Vardoulakis, "Political Theology and the Unworking of Meaning," in *Cultural Critique* 73 (2009): 125.

there seems to be new interest in the place of religion in the modern world, political theology offers new possibilities for charting relationships that cross otherwise hard and fast barriers. It is this that motivates Hent de Vries to argue that political theology "reach[es] further ... upon the central questions of political philosophy and political theory" than other approaches to religion, and offers a "theoretical matrix" supple enough to deal with the great variety of "engagements of religion with the political and politics."[5] And it is this that likewise motivates Slavoj Žižek, Eric Santner, and Kenneth Reinhard to insist that an investigation into the injunction of "neighbor-love not only opens up a set of fundamental issues that continue to define ethical inquiry into modernity but also implies a new theological configuration of political theory."[6] For these and other authors, political theology offers new possibilities for understanding and reconceiving the vexed relationship between religion and politics.[7]

But if political theology can help reconceptualize the complex relations between politics and religion, and has the potential to transcend the normative impetus behind the secular narrative of the evolution of modern society, what is the trade-off for such a view? Is political theology, as de Vries asks, "merely symptomatic of the present difficulty in thinking about the political, politics, and policies ... by turning toward what lies beyond, before, and around them?" Or, does political theology offer us "a different attunement to nonstate actors and actions whose sensibilities, passions, and affects obey a logic and rhythm that eludes the modern understanding of data, numbers, cause, and effect?"[8] For by calling into question basic assumptions about the autonomy of political and religious discourses, political theology can easily seem a backwards step, a regression to a pre-modern constellation of social forces. And yet, for de Vries and others, political

5   Hent de Vries, "Introduction" in *Political Theologies: Public Religions in a Post-Secular World*, eds., Hent de Vries and Lawrence E. Sullivan (New York: Fordham University Press, 2006), 25.

6   Kenneth Reinhard, "Toward a Political Theology of the Neighbor," in *The Neighbor: Three Inquiries into Political Theology*, eds., Slavoj Žižek, Eric L. Santner, and Kenneth Reinhard (Chicago: University of Chicago Press, 2005), 7.

7   Creston Davis, John Milbank, and Slavoj Žižek, eds., *Theology and the Political: The New Debate* (Durham: Duke University Press, 2005).

8   Hent de Vries, "Introduction," op. cit., 9.

theology is not backward-looking in any simple way, complicating as it does simple ideas of progress or regress by showing them to be the product of a certain vision of historical time. It is precisely for this reason, as de Vries points out, that current debates over political theology "remain fragmentary and disoriented," since "the more challenging issues … address a multidimensional space and time before, around, and beyond the 'theologico-political'."[9] Attending to the many and varied imbrications of religion and politics through time, political theology upsets the facile "supersession of the sacred" that structures modern historical consciousness, and thus undermines the assumption that time and history pass ceaselessly without remainder.[10] Not simply an alternative reconstruction of history, political theology interrupts history's very flow by deconstructing the discrete categories known as "politics" and "religion." By helping to reveal, as Kenneth Reinhard puts it, how the "political order is sustained by theological concepts that it cannot completely assimilate," political theology thwarts any simple attempt to render history as a backwards or forwards move away from or towards religion.[11] Instead, it suggests an altogether different temporality, wherein new possibilities for understanding appear as an unconsummated potential of history, something missed in the past. By recalling the persistence of the sacred in the secular, political theology renders incoherent the assumed diachronic passing (and obliteration) of religion into politics. One way to understand renewed interest in political theology, therefore, is to consider how it does something different with time and offers a different way of relating to history.

To better understand this longing for modern history to yield fundamentally different alternatives for thinking about religion and politics, I propose an excursus on nineteenth-century Catholicism. Having served for so long as modern history's other, Catholicism is, in many ways, just the kind of unassimilable remainder that political theology seeks to account for in its recasting of history. Indeed, since the Enlightenment, modernity has rested on deep assumptions about the backwardness of the Roman

9   Ibid., 7.
10 J. G. A. Pocock, "Historiography and Enlightenment: A View of Their History," op. cit., 96.
11 Reinhard, "Toward a Political Theology of the Neighbor," op. cit., 11.

Church, and in this context, the revival of Catholicism after the French Revolution poses a challenge for calibrating modern progress with expectations of its demise. Of course, this essay can offer nothing like an in-depth treatment of Catholic revival in the nineteenth century, and so I confine myself to looking at one particular episode in Germany in 1848.[12] This episode is nevertheless paradigmatic for how the distinct structural pairing of modern/secular against Catholic/regressive meant that any Catholic rejoinder to "modern" trends was always considered *de facto* contrary to the spirit of the times, and so against the flow of history itself. Indeed, it is this pairing that has prevented any serious historical appreciation of the tremendous creativity and fecundity of a Catholicism that, contrary to all expectations, transformed itself into a deeply effective institution combining the seemingly paradoxical virtues of a traditional self-understanding with the tools of modern mass mobilization.[13] By looking at one instance of how that transformation involved a different temporal horizon against which to define Catholic identity, I assess the possibilities of political theology for helping us re-calibrate the way we factor Catholics and similar religious "others" into the modern equation.

To frame this assessment of the possibilities of political theology, I begin with a brief look at how the German political theorist Carl Schmitt appealed to nineteenth-century Catholicism as a touchstone for formulating his conception of political theology. I follow this with a summary of some aspects of the nineteenth-century Catholic revival, and with a more detailed look at how German Catholics responded to the revolutions of 1848. More specifically, I focus on how clergy and laity alike sought to seize what they took to be an unprecedented opportunity for creatively propelling Catholicism into the modern world. By showing how their time-consciousness was constitutive of their sense for the possibilities at hand, I tender the hypothesis that these Catholics were deploying a mode of historical consciousness formative of new kinds of political action, and that this was something

12 For a good overview of the literature on the revival, see David Blackbourn, "The Catholic Church in Europe since the French Revolution: A Review Article," in *Society for Comparative Study of Society and History* 33 (1991).

13 Nicholas Atkin and Frank Tallett, *Priests, Prelates and People: A History of European Catholicism since 1750* (New York: Oxford University Press), 2003.

Schmitt sought to capture in his theorizing. By looking at the way Schmitt appropriated nineteenth-century Catholic political thinking, I must emphasize that my point is not to enter into the debate over the degree to which Schmitt can be considered a Catholic thinker.[14] Instead, my aim is to show how Schmitt understood better than most the distinct power of the Catholic critique of modernity and consequently sought to mobilize its resources, including time and history. I thus do not aim to explain Schmitt's thought by exposing its Catholic roots as much as use him to defamiliarize assumptions about the Catholic past, and show that nineteenth-century Catholics were far from the backwards upstarts they are often portrayed to be. Schmitt's appeal to the nineteenth century was not just a casual plundering of certain relevant texts, but aimed at recuperating strategies for challenging the conviction that modern historical time fixed all possibilities in their place.

Carl Schmitt and Nineteenth-Century Catholicism

In *Political Theology*, first published in 1922, Schmitt contrasted the empty formalism of modern liberal politics with Catholic restoration thought, and declared that "[w]herever Catholic philosophy of the nineteenth century was engaged, it expressed the idea in one form or another that there was now a great alternative that no longer allowed of synthesis." That alternative was only superficially between "Catholicism and atheism," and was in fact a deeper antithesis between "dictatorship" and "everlasting conversation." Surveying the views of Bonald, de Maistre, and Cortes, Schmitt concluded that, "[t]he true significance of those counterrevolutionary philosophers lies precisely in the consistency with which they decide."[15] Their unrelenting decisionism in the face of interminable liberal dialogue expressed the essence of politics. In *Roman Catholicism and Political Form*, Schmitt further explored the continuing relevance of Catholic politics, drawing explicit attention to the "lingering fear of the incomprehensible political power of

---

14 John P. McCormick, *Carl Schmitt's Critique of Liberalism: Against Politics as Technology* (New York: Cambridge University Press, 1997).

15 Carl Schmitt, *Political Theology: Four Chapters on the Concept of Sovereignty*, trans., George Schwab (Chicago: University of Chicago Press, 1985), 53.

Roman Catholicism."[16] In stark contrast with the popular perception of the Church as retrograde, and out of step with the dominant modes of political, economic, and technocratic rationalism, Schmitt asserted that "Catholicism [was] eminently political."[17] Precisely in her "representative character" of the "living Christ," the Church possessed real authority to decide on issues. That the Church could and did "adapt itself to every social and political form" was not a weakness of Catholic doctrine. On the contrary, "the seemingly contradictory political behavior of Catholicism so often reproached is explained by its formal juridical character."[18] As the representative of Christ, the Church was not restricted to the administrative function of carrying out one specific mandate, but was capable as a "juridical person" of creating new law. This put the Church beyond narrow political and ideological categories. It also earned it the scorn of modern society, for as Schmitt observed, "[t]he great betrayal laid to the Catholic Church is that it does not conceive Christ as a private person, does not conceive Christianity as a private matter, something wholly and inwardly spiritual, but rather has given it form as a visible institution.... To the enemy of all forms, this raises the specter of the devil triumphant."[19]

Schmitt's relationship to Catholicism is a topic that has been treated both biographically and systematically in relation to the broader tradition of Catholic political philosophy.[20] Without denying the importance of this work, I must emphasize that I am not asking how being Catholic shaped his thought or how he drew on or rejected official Catholic teachings. Instead, I ask how the example of nineteenth-century Catholicism helped Schmitt formulate key aspects of his political theory: what was it about specific trends in Catholic thought and politics in the nineteenth century that attracted Schmitt? In many ways, his fascination with nineteenth-century Catholics like Bonald, de Maistre, and Cortes seems strangely out of place in the twentieth century—not least because it is typically characterized as

16   Ibid., 3.
17   Ibid., 16.
18   Ibid., 29.
19   Ibid., 32.
20   Manfred Dahlheimer, *Carl Schmitt und der deutsche Katholizismus 1888–1936* (Paderborn: Schöningh, 1998).

a period of triumphant secularization. And yet, this fascination was the touchstone for Schmitt's dictum that "[a]ll significant concepts of the modern theory of the state are secularized theological concepts."[21] Viewed in one way, of course, Schmitt's claim can be seen as de-legitimizing the present for the sake of the past, as Hans Blumenberg has argued.[22] What is seemingly modern is, in fact, really a set of fundamentally medieval ideas repackaged to satisfy the contemporary longing for something new. One can also detect in it a distinct "nostalgia," as Jürgen Habermas points out.[23] But rather than convict it of illegitimacy—of violating the rules of time and history—it seems more appropriate to try and understand the appeal of political theology in this form. To put it simply, why does Schmitt want to see things this way? How is he able to abide this "contemporaneousness of the non-contemporaneous," to use Johann Baptist Metz's memorable phrase?

Part of the answer, it seems to me, has to do with how nineteenth-century Catholicism helped him unmask modernity's self-satisfaction with its own progress. Modern resentment towards the Church was Janus-faced: on the one hand, it rested on the confident assumption that liberalism and other political ideologies had secured for humanity a surer political footing in the this-worldly realities of society as opposed to the ethereal realm of the other-worldly; on the other hand, even the most confident liberal could not overlook the real and persistent fact that the Church had yet to recede into the mists of time. In precise measure as modern liberals were confident that the Church could not hang on much longer, they were mystified by its continuing ability to hang on in the present:

> For the whole of the parliamentary and democratic nineteenth
> century, one most often heard the charge that Catholic politics
> is nothing more than a limitless opportunism. Its elasticity is
> really astounding; it unites with opposing movements and

21 Carl Schmitt, *Political Theology*, op. cit., 36.
22 Hans Blumenberg, *The Legitimacy of the Modern Age*, trans., Robert M. Wallace (Cambridge: MIT Press, 1983), 96.
23 Jürgen Habermas, *Between Naturalism and Religion*, trans., Ciaran Cronin (New York: Polity, 2008), 135.

groups. Thousands of times it has been accused of making common cause with various governments and parties in different countries. Critics have demonstrated how it always pursues political coalitions, whether with absolute monarchs or monarchomachists; how, during the Holy Alliance, after 1815, it became a center of reaction and an enemy of all liberal freedoms, and in other countries an exponent of these same freedoms, especially freedom of the press and freedom of education; how in European monarchies, it preaches the alliance of throne and altar, and in the peasant democracies of the Swiss cantons or in North America it stands wholly on the side of a firm democracy. Men of such eminence as Montalembert, Tocqueville, and Lacordaire represented liberal Catholicism at a time when many of their fellow Catholics still saw in liberalism the Antichrist or at least his forerunner. Catholic royalists and legitimists appear arm-in-arm with Catholic defenders of the republic. Some Catholics are tactically aligned with a socialism, others are believed to be in league with the devil. They have even parlayed with Bolsheviks at a time when bourgeois advocates of the sanctity of private property still saw in them a cabal of criminals *hors la loi*.[24]

What was even more unsettling, of course, was that "this limitless ambiguity combines with the most precise dogmatism and a will to decision as it culminates in the doctrine of papal infallibility."[25] For Schmitt, any seeming political contradiction was only apparent, however. The "essence of the Roman-Catholic *complexio oppositorum* lies in a specific, formal superiority over the matter of human life," not in any particular rule or doctrine as such. Rooted in the consistent "realization of the principle of representation," the Church above all "succeeded in constituting a sustaining configuration of historical and social reality that, despite its formal characteristics, retains its concrete existence."[26]

24   Ibid., 4.
25   Ibid., 8.
26   Ibid.

Schmitt used nineteenth-century Catholic politics to establish a baseline for comparing, contrasting, and ultimately exposing liberal democracy as an empty form lacking substantive content. Liberals celebrated and promoted endless dialogue but were incapable of articulating fundamental principles without referring to other values.[27] Nineteenth-century Catholics, by contrast, were particularly not only convinced—but capable of asserting—a substantive alternative historical vision, and seizing on possibilities otherwise foreclosed by the ideological straitjacket of modernity. That Schmitt found in the nineteenth-century Catholic rejoinder to modernity the most salutary expression of what he sought to explicate as political theology amounted to more than simply challenging clichés about Catholic "backwardness." It involved transcending temporal and historical categories according to whose logic Catholicism could only ever appear as "a phantom of the past."[28] By foregrounding how the Church "succeeded in constituting a sustaining configuration of historical and social reality," Schmitt presented a picture of the Church that was simultaneously inside and outside history: timeless, yet empowered by its sovereignty to take decisive action in any situation regardless of the demands imposed by the march of progress. And he thus urged readers to see in the specific outlines of nineteenth-century Catholicism a resilience to the pressures of time and history that was instructive, even prototypical, for transcending the problems of modern politics. That this resilience drew on a deeper tension between secular time and eschatology in the Christian approach to history, as Jacob Taubes points out, is certainly true.[29] By singling out nineteenth-century Catholicism as the best alternative to the liberal politics of his day, Schmitt demonstrated a particular interest in the capacity of nineteenth-century Catholicism for creative reinvention as critics of modernity. Schmitt's fascination for this particular chapter in Catholic thought motivates me to look closer at this resurgent Catholicism of the nineteenth century. But a caveat is in order

27 John Stroup, "Political Theology and Secularization Theory in Germany 1918–1939: Emanuel Hirsch as a Phenomenon of his Time," in *Harvard Theological Review* 80 (1987): 1–48.

28 Carl Schmitt, *Roman Catholicism and Political Form*, trans., G. L. Ulmen (Westport, Conn.: Greenwood Press, 1996), 35.

29 Jacob Taubes, *From Cult to Culture* (Palo Alto: Stanford University Press, 2010), 12.

first. The following detour into the nineteenth century is intended neither to commend nor excoriate Schmitt as a good or poor student of "real" history. Rather, it is aimed at fostering a better appreciation of how his vision of political theology was nourished by his reading of how Catholics responded to the pressures of modernity.

Catholic Revival in the Nineteenth Century

The French Revolution and its aftermath changed Catholicism in Europe forever.[30] The violent assault on the Church and Catholicism was nothing short of traumatic for contemporaries and, as Austen Ivereigh reminds us, left an indelible mark on the entire nineteenth century that is "easy to forget (because we are too familiar with it)."[31] The loss of the Papal States, imprisonment of Pope Pius VII, forcible suppression of Catholic traditions, attacks against clergy, re-dedication of Churches, and other indignities promoted a sense of urgency among Catholics that they had to do more to defend the faith if these events were not to be repeated. In the German territories, the "Principal Conclusion of the Extraordinary Imperial Delegation" (*Reichsdeputationshauptschluss*) of 1803 dissolved the ecclesiastical states and reorganized the political and ecclesiastical map of central Europe, leading to the transfer of millions into states where others of a different confession now ruled them.[32] Conceived as a way to compensate German princes for territory lost on the left bank of the Rhine, the secularizations of 1803 closed numerous Catholic seminaries and other education and charitable institutions, and scores of religious orders were expelled and had their property

---

30   J. Derek Holmes and Bernard W. Bickers, *A Short History of the Catholic Church* (New York: Burns & Oakes, 1983). See also, Atkins, *Priests, Prelates, and People,* op. cit.

31   Austen Ivereigh, "Introduction: The Politics of Religion in an Age of Revival," in *The Politics of Religion in an Age of Revival. Studies in Nineteenth-Century Europe and Latin America,* ed., Austen Ivereigh (London: Institute of Latin American Studies, 2000). Jeffrey von Arx, "A Post-Traumatic Church. Vatican I and the 'Long 19th Century,'" in *America,* June 22, 2015.

32   For more details, see Rudolf Lill, "Reichskirche – Säkularisation – Katholische Bewegung," in *Der Soziale und Politische Katholizismus. Entwicklungslinien in Deutschland 1803–1963,* ed., Anton Rauscher, vol. 1 (Munich: Olzog, 1981).

appropriated.[33] This affected everything from the teaching of Catholic theology at universities to the local price of beer in the market-place. To some at the time, the Catholic Church seemed destined to collapse altogether. It had, after all, not been able to resist these measures, and though the Papal States were restored at the Congress of Vienna in 1815, their existence was steadily challenged over the course of subsequent decades as the *Risorgimento* united Italians in a new nation state and placed the "Roman Question" on the agenda of European international affairs. To be sure, European leaders saw religion as a key part of their restoration agenda in 1815, and sought to encourage renewed religious devotion. They even allowed the reinstatement of the Jesuits to help reconvert European Catholics back to the faith. However, European leaders made no sincere effort to compensate the Church for its considerable loss of political and economic power, restore the massive loss of land, or reconstruct the ecclesiastical states. They also gave scant attention to the issue of diocesan boundaries thrown into disarray by the Napoleonic wars as they put the finishing touches on their map of the new Europe. After 1815, the Church learned to accommodate itself to a new role on the diplomatic scene, and resign itself to relying on major powers such as Austria and France for its security. So entwined did the Church seem with its status as a sovereign power that, given the steady decline of its temporal power and influence, one can understand why some contemporary observers thought the Church would soon disappear altogether.

And yet, in spite of these losses Catholicism underwent an uneven but steady revival across the German territories and beyond in the decades after 1815.[34] In contrast to the flagging piety of the eighteenth century and the anti-clericalism of the revolutionary period, Catholicism saw distinct improvements over the course of the nineteenth century that included: greater numbers of people attending mass and related observances, growth in the size and number of religious orders, the proliferation of Catholic contrafraternities and other lay associations, an increased prominence of women in religious orders and lay associations, and an expanded

33 E. E. Y Hales, *Revolution and the Papacy 1769–1846* (London: Eyre & Spottiswoode, 1960).

34 Blackbourn, "The Catholic Church in Europe since the French Revolution: A Review Article," op. cit.

Catholic press.[35] This revival was, to a very large extent, grassroots, and was not the result of a coordinated plan on the part of the Church hierarchy, who struggled at times to corral this surge in popular sentiment. Though slow to accept these changes, Church leaders capitalized on the opportunities made possible by the new piety and gradually transformed mass popular support into a base for stronger leadership. Training better and more committed priests, expanding the number and kind of religious orders, and encouraging a "cult of personality" around the pope, the Church asserted more power over faith and morals in direct proportion to its loss of temporal power. Though the revolution and its aftermath was an unmitigated disaster for the Church in many ways, it is clear in retrospect that no event did more to shift the focus to Rome as the heart of Catholicism. Though it dramatically altered the Church's formal alliance with political power, the French Revolution effectively "removed the obstacles raised by the *Ancien Régime* in absolutist Europe," giving Rome unprecedented influence to reorder the Church over the course of subsequent decades.[36] The dissolution of many wealthy bishoprics, monasteries, and abbeys did much to displace the nobility from the clergy and open the road for members of the lower classes to move into the higher ecclesiastical ranks. And as the nobility came to exert less influence through these positions, Rome was able exert more uniform control over the clergy.[37] To be sure, there were countervailing forces. The fact that the lower clergy came increasingly from the non-noble classes created its own headaches. After all, these clergy were in a position to support and more effectively work alongside lay persons in the new Catholic associations and organizations that emerged during the nineteenth century, and undertook initiatives not always in line with what Church officials wanted. They also played a role in the Church's pivoting towards its important intervention in the "social question."[38] But unlike the nobility

35 Nicholas Atkin and Frank Tallett, *Priests, Prelates and People: A History of European Catholicism Since 1750,* op. cit.

36 Klaus Schatz, *Papal Primacy: From Its Origins to the Present* (Liturgical Press, 1996), 144.

37 Marvin R. O'Connell, "Ultramontanism and Dupanloup: The Compromise of 1865," in *Church History* 53 (1984): 200–04.

38 J. Derek Holmes and Bernard Bickers, *Short History of the Catholic Church,* op. cit.

who once held these offices, the new clergy were not partisan defenders of inherited wealth and power and therefore not inclined to think of themselves as a counterweight to Roman aspirations. On the contrary, they were much more likely to view themselves as deriving their mission from a Church conceived almost unilaterally in Roman terms.

With the decline of its political and economic power, and disencumbered of the various counter-weights to its authority embedded in the *Ancien Régime*, the nineteenth-century Church was in a position to assert itself more forcefully in the realm of family, faith, and morals. This change went hand in hand with a new focus on women in the Church. The dramatic increase in the size and number of female religious orders, the rise in Marian devotion (culminating in the dogmatization of Mary's "immaculate conception" in 1854), and the overall elevation of the moral authority of mothers and wives was part of a broader "feminization of religion" in the nineteenth century that saw women exert a new and different kind of influence on society through their religious activities.[39] It also went hand in hand with significant changes in the communications networks linking Catholics in far-flung reaches of the globe, as Catholicism became mediatized in new ways. Both clergy and laity learned to master new modes of communication and publicity, and explored new possibilities for framing a vision of contemporary Catholicism. In this, Catholic scholars often vied with Rome over who spoke in the name of Catholicism in the public sphere. Of course, no stranger to conflict with its members, the Church reserved to itself the right to define the nature of the faith and to police the boundaries of what did and did not count as "Catholic." But if the Church was consistent to a fault in rejecting certain ideas as dangerous to orthodoxy, it was not always clear how to contain the energies of popular Catholicism or how to navigate the new and shifting social, political, and cultural landscape. In this context, scholars and other men of letters often claimed to be better situated and better able to diagnose the times than their ecclesiastical overseers, and their suggestions for how to navigate the shifting landscape frequently brought them into conflict with Church authority.

39 Patrick Pasture and Jan Art, *Beyond the Feminization Thesis: Gender and Christianity in Modern Europe* (Leuven University Press, 2012).

Sweeping change created a space for the emergence of what Gene Burns has identified as the "ideological history of the modern Catholic Church." By this, what Burns means is the evolution of a set of more or less ad hoc strategies for competing with the welter of new ideas. As "the papacy came to gradually de-emphasize doctrine that had specific, controversial implications for state policy," and by embracing a populist foundation, Rome positioned itself to be the "exclusive authority over faith and morals of Catholic individuals and families as the basis of its religious authority."[40] This turn to ideology notwithstanding, Burns cautions against construing this in overly narrow political terms or "classifying its components according to such categories as 'left' and 'right'." Instead, he urges us to view ideology as a set of "belief[s] developed and maintained through social interaction" that help enable a range of "understandings and priorities that pattern ... social participation." Viewed in this way, ideological Catholicism "always include[d] various spaces of autonomy" and was thus "always potentially an object of political struggle" precisely to the extent that various factions fought to secure "a hierarchy of issues enforced through the exercise of power."[41] And though the outcome of this contest was a model of centralized Church authority in Rome and in the papacy, it is essential to understand that this outcome was neither predestined to happen, nor was it a process that one should construe as rooted in willful indifference to the needs or wishes of "the people." On the contrary, centralization of authority in the Roman pontiff was the contingent result of a battle for control and a desire to contain, and then capitalize on, the new groundswell of popular Catholicism. In this way, the "new Catholicism" that emerged in the course of the nineteenth century was thus paradoxically a product of centrifugal and centripetal forces, both of which pulled it away from the old regime. As Vincent Viaene demonstrates in his analysis of the Catholic revival, liberal politics, and the creation of the Belgian state, the Church's growing appreciation for popular opinion over the course of the nineteenth century was instrumental in re-legitimating the Church as a transnational institution. That it did so based on popular

40 Gene Burns, *The Frontiers of Catholicism: The Politics of Ideology in a Liberal World* (Berkeley: University of California Press, 1994).
41 Ibid., 13.

support points to how "[p]opular Catholicism was ... constitutive of modernity."[42]

A watershed was reached in 1838, when the Prussian government arrested and imprisoned Count Droste zu Vischering, Archbishop of the diocese of Cologne. When they sanctioned his election in 1835, the government hoped that the aging Droste zu Vischering would want to avoid confrontation over the increasingly sensitive issue of mixed marriages between Catholics and Protestants. The official Catholic position held that such marriages required permission and that all children from the marriage would be raised in the Catholic faith. In practice, however, the rule had been softened. The new Archbishop decided to stand firm on the Church's position and entered into a long battle with Prussian officials culminating in his arrest and imprisonment in 1837. Reaction to this event, which came to be known as the "Cologne Troubles," was decisive. Demonstrations took place, the Vatican condemned the arrest, and a pamphlet war denounced Protestant-Prussian aggression. In this context, popular support for the Archbishop did not merely express indignation at the violation of religious boundaries, but yielded new forms of social and political protest.[43] One of these strategies was to denounce the attack as a breach of federal law, a perspective forcefully articulated by Joseph Görres in his tract, *Athanasius*, published in 1837. A former republican and supporter of the revolution, he defended Catholics' right to attack the Prussian government publicly, and insisted that such criticism was neither disloyal nor treasonous.[44] He justified Droste zu Vischering's handling of the situation from three different perspectives. First, as Archbishop, Droste zu Vischering was bound to the rules, precepts, and hierarchy of the Church he represented. His duty therefore lay in defending Church law. Second, as a subject of the Prussian monarch, he was also bound by the law of the land and required to obey all civil acts of legislation that did not touch on matters of religion. This

---

42 Vincent Viaene, *Belgium and the Holy See from Gregory XVI to Pius IX, 1831–1859: Catholic Revival, Society and Politics in 19th-Century Europe* (Rome: Belgisch Historisch Instituutte, 2001).

43 Thomas Nipperdey, *Germany from Napoleon to Bismarck* (Princeton, N.J.: Princeton University Press, 1996), 4.

44 Ibid.

obligated him to defend federal statutes guaranteeing religious freedom. Third, as a representative of his confession, Droste zu Vischering was bound by conscience. His duty therefore lay in living up to what he believed as a member of the Catholic faith, publicly and without regard for threats of illegal persecution. This readiness to act publicly in the name of the faith, which Görres defiantly celebrated in the figure of the Archbishop, helped form the crucible of the revival mentality. *Athanasius* thus became, as Thomas Nipperdey characterized it, a veritable "charter for political Catholicism," which "popularised, simplified, emphasized, and polarized, with great rhetorical feeling the concrete legal issues involved, and transformed them into a matter of principle."[45] Along with hundreds of other pamphlets, it helped transform confessional polemics into a program for political action, mobilizing both clerics and laymen to found distinct Catholic institutions and organizations, promote the Catholic press, and revamp Catholic scholarship.

One of the most striking features of the revival was a resurgence in popular religion that contrasted markedly with the waning of such practices in the eighteenth century. One of the most dramatic expressions of popular piety occurred in 1844 when perhaps as many as a quarter of a million pilgrims, most of them from rural areas, travelled to visit the Holy Coat of Trier—said to be Jesus's own robe. The pilgrims consisted mostly of farmers and small trades-people, as well as clerics and a portion of the Catholic aristocracy. The event was not universally welcomed by all Catholics however, especially the Catholic bourgeoisie, who lamented that the event only strengthened those who criticized Catholic backwardness. Even the Church hierarchy was concerned that the event might get out of control. As Wolfgang Schieder has shown, the 1844 exhibition was different from previous exhibitions not only in size, but in kind. Unlike the majority of pilgrimages taking place across the German territories in the preceding decades, this was a "pilgrimage from above" that sought to channel and control Catholic sentiment. In the wake of the Cologne Troubles and other unrest, both the ecclesiastical hierarchy and Prussian administrators had an interest in curbing spontaneous—and potentially dangerous—gatherings. According to Schieder, therefore, the Trier pilgrimage represented a new conservative

45   Ibid., 371.

alliance between Church and state.[46] And yet, if his analysis tells us a lot about how administrators and ecclesiastical officials viewed the pilgrimage, I think it overlooks other, equally important consequences. For one thing, by focusing on how the pilgrimage was stage-managed from on high, Schieder perhaps unwittingly falls prey to the prejudice that pilgrims did what priests and other officials told them to, and by implication, that they believed in the authenticity of the robe without any misgivings. Indeed, he states in no uncertain terms that "the pilgrimage was undertaken in a collective way by individual pilgrims, and not reflectively thought through."[47] And yet, if bishops, clerics, and a large number of the Catholic bourgeoisie doubted the authenticity of the robe, why couldn't the pilgrims entertain similar misgivings even as they took to the road to see for themselves? In his analysis of the popular prayer books sold at the exhibition, Schieder himself observes how they focused obsessively on the authenticity of the robe. Why do so if, as he says, "the pilgrim believed without a doubt ... that the exhibited material was the last article of clothing belonging to the historical Jesus?"[48] Why do so, if one could take for granted that the uneducated pilgrim already (and always) believed in miracles? The very proliferation of this literature suggests that pilgrims may have harbored similar doubts about the robe as their more educated counterparts. At the very least, it suggests that they were more ambivalent than Schieder allows, and confirms what many scholars today argue, and that is, that popular religiosity needs to be grasped as a multivalent phenomenon that offers different, and even conflicting, possibilities of practice.[49]

Debates over the robe's authenticity and over the veneration of relics more generally raised important questions about the very meaning and definition of "Catholic" practices. If, for many, the robe was unquestionably Jesus' own, it is important to note that a good number of clerics, journalists, and other members of the Catholic bourgeoisie openly doubted the authenticity

46 Wolfgang Schieder, "Kirche Und Revolution: Sozialgeschichtliche Aspekte der Trierer Wallfahrt Von 1844," in *Archiv für Sozialgeschichte* 14 (1974): 419–54.

47 Ibid., 446.

48 Ibid., 451.

49 Robert Orsi, *Between Heaven and Earth: The Religious Worlds that People Make and the Scholars Who Study Them* (Princeton: Princeton University Press, 2005).

of the robe and lamented its exhibition.[50] Indeed, bourgeois opposition to the pilgrimage even spawned a breakaway "German-Catholic" movement that grew to an estimated eighty thousand members. Led by the priest Johannes Ronge, the German-Catholics attacked the pilgrimage for encouraging and exploiting superstition and called for a "battle to cleanse German Catholic worship of superstitious practices."[51] In their *Basic Principles and Articles*, the German-Catholics denounced confession, celibacy, relics and icons, and the primacy of the papacy. Defending the "healthy reason of the masses," they aimed to "mak[e] the content of the faith part of a living, contemporary cognition."[52] Though their views ultimately put them outside of the fold, it is important to recognize that the German-Catholics emerged just as much from within the matrix of devotional activism as the Trier pilgrims.[53] No less than the pilgrims they criticized, they felt empowered to act in the name of the faith and saw "Catholic life" as the goal of the movement, the objective to be won. This polarization of the faithful is indicative of the stresses and strains of a community that was finding its feet as a political entity.

The massive turnout at Trier and later at various sites of alleged Marian apparitions signaled a potential for mass organization and a readiness among the rank and file to take a decidedly public and political stand in the name of the faith. But popular religious revival did more than rejuvenate Catholic piety. It transformed Catholicism into a resource for identity and action. As Jonathan Sperber put it, in his path-breaking *Popular Catholicism in Nineteenth-Century Germany*, popular religion offered Catholics a way to use "their received cultural heritage, the means they knew of expression and association, in order to oppose or to adapt to changes in their social

50 Wolfgang Schieder, "Kirche Und Revolution: Sozialgeschichtliche Aspekte der Trierer Wallfahrt Von 1844," op. cit., 446.

51 Michaela Tomaschewsky, "Dress Rehearsal for 1848: Johannes Ronge and the German Catholic Movement," in *Consortium on Revolutionary Europe, 1750 –1850* (1994): 117.

52 *Allgemeine Grundsätze und Bestimmungen der Deutsch-Katholischen Kirche wie Sie bei dem ersten Concil in Leipzig an dem Oster-Feste 1845 Berathen und Angenommenn Wurden* (Leipzig: Friedrich Krähe, 1845), 3.

53 Andreas Holzem, *Kirchenreform und Sektenstiftung. Deutschkatholiken, Reformkatholiken und Ultramontane am Oberrhein 1844–1866* (Paderborn: Schöningh, 1994).

environment occurring beyond their conscious control. Their resulting actions transformed, often without conscious intent, both social and political structures and the cultural framework used to interpret them."[54] In his analysis of the apparitions of the Virgin Mary at Marpingen, David Blackbourn likewise points to how popular religion offered Catholics, especially the most vulnerable, an idiom for expressing criticism of both local and regional authorities and anxiety over the pace of social change.[55] These studies, and more besides, have done much to recast our understanding of the Catholic revival.[56] They help us see that, "far from being atavistic survivals, beliefs in the supernatural mediated the far-reaching social and economic changes associated with the process of industrialization and national integration" in the nineteenth century.[57] And they also help us understand how popular Catholicism served as an important factor in how the Church recast itself on new foundations. Their point of departure is that what is significant about Catholic devotional practices is not how in or out of place they may have seemed in the middle of the nineteenth century, but rather how they helped Catholics define themselves in a period of rapid and decisive change. Precisely because they clashed with emerging norms radiating out from centers of social, cultural, and political power, popular religious practices served as weapons for the marginal, disposed, and powerless.

All this suggests that nineteenth-century Catholicism cannot be reduced to a mere ingredient of political reaction or a source of comfort during turbulent times, but was a complex phenomenon that undercuts stark oppositions like backward/progressive and modern/traditional. It also suggests the fruitfulness of conceptualizing these, and other, instances of profoundly public action in the name of the faith as "devotional activism."[58]

---

54 Jonathan Sperber, *Popular Catholicism in Nineteenth-Century Germany* (Princeton University Press, 1984), 1.

55 David Blackbourn, *Marpingen: Apparitions of the Virgin Mary in Nineteenth-Century Germany* (Knopf, 1994).

56 Anders Jarlert, *Piety and Modernity* (Leuven University Press, 2012).

57 Caroline Ford, "Religion and Popular Culture in Modern Europe," *The Journal of Modern History* 65:1 (March 1, 1993): 152–75.

58 Richard Schaefer, "Program for a New Catholic Wissenschaft: Devotional Activism and Catholic Modernity in the Nineteenth Century," in *Modern Intellectual History* 4 (2007): 432.

Not restricted to Catholics, or even to members of formal religious institutions, devotional activism refers to how religious actors (taken broadly)
mold themselves—often in ways both unconscious and unintentional—
to the circumstances and patterns cast by opponents. There exists a deep
structural affinity between religious actors and their critics, one borne of
competition, that involves innovative and public modes of self-assertion
that cannot be reduced to a static understanding of culture as tradition.
Devotional activism presupposes that identities are never fixed, but only
ever appear in action. Rather than always being clear to every participant,
the motives driving devotional activism are rooted in the diffuse presuppositions of the "lifeworld."[59] Though broadly shared and even taken for
granted, these motives require clarification under new circumstances.[60] It
is precisely this combination of certainty and uncertainty about these presuppositions that gives devotional activism its particular urgency at any
particular moment. A useful corrective to the tendency to see particular
"religious" identity (e.g., Catholic, Jewish, religious, Muslim etc.) as a
transparent value understood by everyone in the same way, and thus the
incontestable and unproblematic root of "revival" or "reaction," devotional
activism lets us see better how actors contest the world that enables and
encompasses their actions. In the case of the structural transformation of
the Church from one based on territorial sovereignty to one based on popular support, devotional activism played a pivotal role in redefining the
nature of the Church and Catholicism, and lets us see how Catholics

59   First introduced by Edmund Husserl to discuss the naïve embeddedness of a
     person in his or her environment, "lifeworld" refers to the knowledge that is
     taken for granted before it becomes the focus of thematic (theoretical) atten-
     tion in the "world." In his appropriation of the concept, Jürgen Habermas has
     translated this idea of the naïve embeddedness of the lifeworld in terms of the
     discursive conditions underwriting communicative action. According to
     Habermas, the lifeworld consists in the "more or less diffuse, always unprob-
     lematic, background convictions" that serve as a "source of situation defini-
     tions … presupposed by participants as unproblematic" in communication.
     See Jürgen Habermas, *The Theory of Communicative Action. Lifeworld and Sys-
     tem: A Critique of Functionalist Reason*, trans., Thomas McCarthy, vol. 2
     (Boston: Beacon Press, 1987), 335.
60   Ibid., 131.

explicitly adopted the organizational techniques of their non-Catholic foes. This meant, above all, publicly expressing and defending Catholic identity and action in the stark light of evolving rules governing civil society. In view of the new and rapidly evolving avenues of communication and publication, taking a principled, public, and explicitly "Catholic" position on specific issues was a salutary way for Catholics to recognize themselves as a political force. Just how devotional activism shaped Catholicism into a movement—in light of which being Catholic took on a whole new meaning—can be illustrated in more detail with respect to the revolutions of 1848.

Catholics and the Revolutions of 1848

The revolutions of 1848 were decisive for European Catholics. The collapse of the European Catholic establishment that began in France in February 1848 and culminated in the Pope's retreat from Rome in January 1849 forced Catholics to rethink their place in the new political landscape. This landscape was defined, in most cases, by new legislation disestablishing the Church from any privileged position in the political order, but simultaneously granting it unprecedented autonomy to decide its own future. In the German territories, the Archbishop of Cologne, Johannes von Geissel, invited his fellow bishops to an emergency meeting in Würzburg in October 1848 to assess the situation. In a *Promemoria* circulated before the meeting, von Geissel stressed what was fast becoming a familiar refrain, namely, that "a new age is beginning, and with it a new order of things."[61] The new order might remain or it might not. If it did, however, Geissel cautioned that Catholics should reconcile themselves to a constitutional separation between Church and state. During the meeting, the bishops were chiefly preoccupied with practical issues. They debated at length what position they should take on Catholic education, the training of priests, and the maintenance of Church property and wealth, as well as the question of what to say about the separation of Church and state, in principle, and what their

61 Jürgen Brandt, *Eine Katholische Universität in Deutschland? Das Ringen Der Katholiken in Deutschland Um Eine Universitätsbildung Im 19. Jahrhundert* (Köln: Böhlau, 1981), 144.

official position should be towards other Christians and Jews.[62] In their joint statement, however, what stands out is not just their rather surprising endorsement of certain key tenets of religious freedom, but rather a confidence that history was on their side, no matter what the political situation: "In stormy times, when the surges of unbridled passion might ignite in wildfire, nations rise against nations in fights over their existence, and the foundations of civil and state order sway, eighteen hundred years proves that it is the Church … that has raised and civilized the people."[63] Echoing this same faith in history, Bishop Wilhelm Freiherr von Ketteler used an Advent sermon to stress that Catholics could rely on the teaching authority of the Church precisely because the Church stood outside time. Not only in troubled times, but in all times, the teaching authority of the Church stood as the best defense against being slave to public opinion. "If we ask, where this higher infallible authority is, we are then confronted with the great and noteworthy fact that in all of world history there has only been one institution on the whole earth that satisfies our souls' need for peace."[64]

How should we read and interpret the claim that the Church stood outside of time? To see things that way is to see things very differently than non-Catholic contemporaries did. Should we take what Catholics said at face value? Isn't doing so uncritical? To many critics at the time, claims to stand outside of time was nothing more than reactionary rhetoric and did nothing to dissuade them from the plain fact that the Church was confronted with a singular choice: accommodating to the times, or fleeing from them in a backwards regression. Thus, for Johann Ferdinand Neigebaur, a determined critic of the "papal empire," the notion of standing outside of time was ludicrous. "Since such a faith can hardly withstand the progress of recent times," those allied with that faith would only ever seek to "return" to the time of "castles, cathedrals, and abbeys," when there were "no highways, let alone railways, and the farmer was beholden to follow the

---

62 For more on Catholic approaches to these issues, see Dagmar Herzog, *Intimacy and Exclusion: Religious Politics in Pre-Revolutionary Baden* (Princeton: Princeton University Press, 1996).

63 *Verhandlungen der ersten Versammlung des katholischen Vereines Deutschlands am 3. 4. 5. und 6. October zu Main* (Mainz: Kirchheim & Schott, 1848), 15.

64 Wilhelm Freiherr von Ketteler, *Die grossen sozialen Fragen der Gegenwart* (Mainz: Grünewald Verlag, 1948), 118.

knight."[65] And yet, given the obviously hostile tenor of this particular perspective, should we not also question whether it is right to take Neigebaur at face value? The truth is, of course, that for too long, historians have accepted the way critics like Neigebaur framed the situation because they have shared its particular view of history and the march of progress. Does seeking to redress that now mean one is obliged to accept uncritically the Catholic version of events? The answer, of course, is no, if that means affirming its explicit content or claiming to occupy a privileged position outside of history. But that does not mean one can't take the claim itself seriously, or attempt to place it within a distinctly Catholic set of judgments about the world and the course of history. Without denying that it can be difficult at times to "see things their way," it is essential that we not let ourselves be dissuaded from making the effort, especially when this involves upholding dubious ideas about progress and regress in history.[66] One of the possibilities that political theology offers for recasting the fate of religion in modern history is to leverage the belated recognition of certain possibilities from the past against this type of narrow historical vision.

Not only bishops, but also rank and file Catholics were aware times were changing. This was expressed in no uncertain terms by delegates to the first Meeting of Catholic Societies convened in Mainz in October 1848. In the opening speech of the meeting, Joseph Mast decried attempts to label him and other Catholics "followers of the old system." Rejecting the mantle of "reaction," he argued that no one had "suffered more" under the "bureaucracy" of the old system than Catholics. He unambiguously declared, "our direction is not backwards, but forwards."[67] Franz Joseph Buß, professor at the University of Freiburg and president of the meeting, echoed this faith in an open future, charging delegates with the task of "sowing into life the fruitful seeds of the future."[68] Johannes Sepp even went so far as to compare the situation with the dawn of creation itself, declaring "we

---

65 Johann Ferdinand Neigebaur, *Der Papst und sein Reich* (Leipzig: Arnold Ruge Verlagsbureau, 1848), 409.

66 Alister Chapman, John Coffey, and Brad Gregory, eds., *Seeing Things Their Way: Intellectual History and the Return of Religion.*

67 *Verhandlungen*, 24.

68 Ibid., 41.

stand again before a decisive change in the times, where the passage from the story of creation is once again applicable: 'And there was evening, and there was morning. One day.' What happens in such moments is decisive and strikes the roots of the future" (Sepp 66). How should we interpret these appeals to time? On the one hand, of course, recognizing that a new age has arrived can be read as adopting a pragmatic and even progressive attitude towards changing realities. In other words, it means accommodating to the times. On the other hand, it can be read as a rallying cry to a new version of an old fight; to wit, in this new age there is a new set of obstacles that can and must be overcome in the same way Catholics had done so often in the past. But the concern for time can also be read in a third way, construing the reference to time as less an index of backwards or forwards—less as a variable—than as the objective to be won. In a revolutionary context, declaring oneself to be on the edge of a new era can be taken to express a profound feeling of being called to act with or against the times. Yet it can also be taken to express a feeling that time itself is not right; that it must be renewed, conquered, or even begun again. In this context, it is important to distinguish between what happens in time and using time to render events intelligible. This is a distinction Giorgio Agamben makes with regard to the messianic time of Pauline theology, namely, that there is a distinction to be made between what happens in time and what time itself can do, what it achieves for us when we construe it in specific ways and thereby become conscious of it:

> While our representation of chronological time, or the time *in* which we are, separates, divides us from ourselves, and makes us the powerless spectators of ourselves, observing in (without time) the time that runs away from us, messianic time, or operational time, in which we grasp and accomplish, is the time that we *are*, and for that reason, the only real time, the only time that we *have*.[69]

From this perspective, my point is to suggest that part of the Catholic agenda in 1848 was to seize and turn to their advantage revolutionary time,

---

69   Giorgio Agamben, "The Time That Is Left," in *Epoché* VII (2002), 5.

and that this was part of a larger and explicit strategy to seize the weapons of their opponents. If the revolution portended a decisive break with the past, the champions of progress were quick to seize on this rupture as further confirmation of what they already assumed was the otherwise immutable march of time. But for Catholics confronted with the challenge of translating their tradition into the new idiom of constitutional rights and institutional autonomy, the revolution was as much about seizing and turning to their advantage revolutionary time that could serve them.

The Mainz Meeting called together representatives from the newly founded Pius Associations from across the German territories. Founded during the early stages of the revolution and promoted throughout the German lands through the influential journal *The Catholic*, these associations promoted the cause of religious freedom as a politically expedient tool for defending Catholic interests.[70] On the vanguard of Catholic action that I have sought to explicate as devotional activism, the meeting served as a forum for knitting diverse experiences into a collective sensibility. One after another, delegates to the meeting described the specific local means employed to overcome various inequities in recent years. Such means include a renewal of scholarship, petition campaigns, missions, political organization, temperance, and the founding of religious houses. More than mere commiseration, this concerted effort to affirm the unity of Catholic action across time and space helped further politicize Catholicism according to a distinctly new strategy. This strategy consisted above all in turning to Catholic advantage whatever instruments of power lay at hand, regardless of origin or their association with dreaded foes. President of the Meeting, Franz Joseph Buß, summarized this strategy as follows: "Since the times are extraordinary, so must be the means." It was crucial to "use the tools that we have learned from our opponents.... Let us go to his lair, seek out the enemy, and there find a well-run organization."[71] According to Buß, Catholics must learn to apply the techniques of their enemies especially in such areas as education, the press, science and scholarship, politics, and the social question. The "time was not yet past" when Catholics could influence the entire course of the future. Though the present situation may demand an especially vigilant "moral censorship"

70 Sperber, *Popular Catholicism*, op. cit.
71 *Verhandlungen*, 74.

against bad and corrupting influences, this could not be achieved in the old way by preventing their public circulation. Instead, according to Buß, the most effective way of promoting Catholic interests was through the ballot. Only in this way could Catholics hope to atone for their share in the failings of the past and recoup lost opportunities in the name of a fresh start: "[I]t falls to us to recoup what has been lost. There is an absolute responsibility that flows through world history. We must shoulder the burden that we and our immediate predecessors have incurred."[72] No less than Schmitt, Buß understood that history itself needed to be re-taken from those who would exclude Catholics from it. To the degree that progress in history seemingly excluded Catholic self-assertion almost in principle, he urged Catholics to not let themselves be boxed into a situation in which they could no longer call on their own past to effectively shore up their position in the present.

For delegates to the Mainz Meeting, the overriding objective was to legitimate new strategies and sanction specific modes of political action that would advance the Catholic cause under new circumstances. This not only produced a heightened sense of time and a mission in history, but more importantly confirmed Catholics in their ability to make history. Reflecting on the situation only three years earlier, Heinrich von Andlaw lamented how the Badenese petition campaign of 1845 had been limited precisely because of a "lack of mutual acquaintance" among Catholics across the German territories. In view of the new relationships forged by the meeting, however, von Andlaw foresaw the dawning of a new age:

> We ask, whether that segment of the *Volk* animated by a Catholic consciousness is not just as able to take a stand, whether it is not also allowed to fight politically to realize its ideals?... That we are assembled here in such numbers signals important progress, parallel to the progress in German national feeling.[73]

By construing the politicization of Catholicism as a force equal to "progress in German national feeling"—one of the primary temporal indices of

72 Ibid., 77.
73 Ibid., 55.

modernity—von Andlaw here summarized perhaps better than anyone the transformation of Catholicism into a timely and legitimate participant in the battle of ideologies. This was not an *ad hoc* response, but reflected a broader devotional activism that turned secular tools to Catholic advantage. This is reflected in von Andlaw's view that the separation of Church and state did not have to entail a "break, or a severing of the living ties that bind Church and state."[74] Indeed, that was impossible in several respects. For one thing, it was in the nature of the Church that it "must penetrate all facets of life." And moreover, how could one divide in an individual the part belonging to Church and the part belonging to state? For von Andlaw, these considerations made it impractical to take literally the notion of the separation of Church and state. He therefore suggested that the separation of Church and state was best understood as "standing on one's own feet" against existing "governments" in the name of Catholic interests. Viewed in this way, Catholic associations like those assembled at Mainz might then "promote the education of humanity … without which there can be no hope of lasting respect for the law.[75]

The Mainz Meeting gave Catholics a sense for themselves as a movement in history as effective as any political foe. Though overlooked by many, then and since, this politicization of Catholicism was not lost on Wilhelm Riehl, one of the most perceptive commentators on the social situation at the time. Analyzing the social changes leading up to the revolutions of 1848, Riehl argued that Catholics were far from the backwards upstarts they were often portrayed to be. On the contrary, in 1848, it was "[t]he Protestants [who] considered how … one could make the least dangerous compromises to the spirit of the times, while the Catholics … asked how the Church might best capitalize on the compromises of the age."[76] The significance of this insight is easily overlooked if one sees Catholics as simply sacrificing principles to pragmatism. We must therefore learn to recognize that the question is not how Catholics (or Jews, Protestants, Muslims, etc.) managed to effect a successful transition to modernity, as though

74 Ibid., 56.
75 Ibid., 57.
76 Wilhelm Riehl, *Die naturgeschichte des volkes als grundlage einer deutschen social-politik* (Berlin: Cotta, 1866), 325.

the burden is somehow on the religious to accommodate to "real" conditions of modern life and society. The question is, rather, how Catholics (and others) co-constituted modernity in and through multiple avenues.

Conclusion

This sketch of the German Catholic revival suggests a different way of understanding Schmitt's fascination with nineteenth-century Catholicism: not as a set of discrete influences on his thinking that can be charted as so many links in a chain, but as an affinity for a particular kind of protest against those who would consign religion to the margins of modern life. To be sure, Schmitt's preference for seeing the Church as a monolithic structure whose head governed its limbs hardly squares with the picture of revival and structural transformation I have sketched here. But this only helps to underscore the larger question of why he appealed to this history, and not another, in his workup of political theology. Schmitt saw in nineteenth-century Catholicism the purest expression of politics, a perception that was less a true recounting of history than a desire for a specific way of dealing with history. The conclusion I draw from this is that Schmitt was attracted to nineteenth-century Catholicism precisely because it was in temporal and historical flux, yet confident in its ability to "constitute," as he so adroitly observed, "a sustaining configuration of historical and social reality."[77] The ability to exert sovereign power—to define the terms of the situation—was commensurate with an ability to decide one's fate in time, and even to master time itself.[78] What Schmitt overlooked, of course, was the fact that much of the power of nineteenth-century Catholic thought derived from a revival movement that was as much a challenge to the power of the Church hierarchy as it was an instrument in their hands. Though he may have wanted to dispel the popular perception of Catholicism as opportunistic, such perceptions weren't altogether wrong. The success of the Catholic revival was predicated on a willingness to seize the advantage wherever and whenever it presented itself, even in the deepest recesses of historical consciousness.

77 Schmitt, *Roman Catholicism and Political Form*, op. cit., 8.
78 Vardoulakis, "Political Theology and the Unworking of Meaning," op. cit., 134.

Convinced that a new age was beginning in 1848, Catholics wanted to turn time to their advantage, building what they took to be viable links between their past—construed less as constraint than as a resource or an enabling condition—and a political future they could call their own. It was this brazen confidence that Catholics had in their ability to make their own history that Schmitt seized on to define political theology. If their devotional activism helped provide a different temporal overture for politicizing Catholicism, then it was those mystic chords that drew Schmitt to these dissenters of the nineteenth century.

What does this mean for our understanding of the resurgent interest in political theology today? To be clear, I do not think it supports any effort to re-read Schmitt's work on behalf of the National Socialist regime in a more positive light. I also do not think that it supports any particular effort to rehabilitate Carl Schmitt as a prophetic voice whose entire *corpus* might be recast as a how-to manual for the twenty-first century. Indeed, following Dominick LaCapra, I think one should be wary of how appeals to political theology can sometimes indulge a disconcerting apocalyptic strain of critical theory.[79] But if we want to better understand the ways that religious people mobilize their faith for various broadly political purposes—today and in the past—then it is crucial that we broaden our perspective to include devotional activism as a mode of self-assertion that is not reducible to traditionalism. In this regard, Schmitt's fascination with nineteenth-century Catholicism is especially instructive. One simply cannot tell the story of Schmitt without taking a very different approach to what Catholics were doing. This does not mean valorizing what they were doing, and it does not mean foregoing the careful and critical study of history. But it does mean understanding that the explicitly religious ideas they had about themselves and their place in history cannot be ignored. Schmitt thus offers a compelling example for thinking differently about religion and politics, one that contributes to our growing awareness of the hidden metaphysical dimensions of modern history. As Claude Lefort shows, the constitution of the "irreversibility of the course of history" in the wake of the cataclysm of the French Revolution engaged in its own efforts to make "history a

---

79 Dominick LaCapra, *History, Literature, Critical Theory* (Ithaca: Cornell University Press, 2013).

mystery" by revealing the nation or society to be the sacred core of history.[80] If the return of political theology has taught us anything, it is that the historical "disavowal of a hidden part of social life"—that is to say, the continuing close relation between religion and politics—sustains the "permanence of the theologico-political" in the interstices of the major streams of social and political life.[81]

---

80 Claude Lefort, "The Permanence of the Theologico-Political?" in *Political Theologies: Public Religions in a Post-Secular World*, eds., Hent. de Vries and Lawrence E. Sullivan (New York: Fordham University Press, 2006), 182.
81 Ibid., 150.

CHAPTER THREE

CATHOLICS AND THE FIRST WORLD WAR:
RELIGION, CULTURE, AND BARBARISM

In 1915, "The Catholic Committee for French Propaganda Abroad" published a collection of essays titled *The German War and Catholicism*.[1] Edited by Monsignor Alfred Baudrillart, Rector of the Catholic Institute of Paris, the collection aimed to win support for the French cause among Catholics in neutral countries, especially the United States. Published with the approval of the Archbishops of Reims and Paris, and no fewer than ten other French bishops, the book did not come from the margin, but from the mainstream of French Catholic life. It was translated into English, Spanish, German, and Italian, and elicited not one but two published responses by German Catholics. What makes these texts significant is that, together, they advanced a fierce debate over the nature of culture and conflict, and help illuminate specifically Catholic responses to the war. Analyzing this debate thus promises to give us a sense for how Catholics negotiated faith and fidelity to the nation, and to deepen our understanding of the role of religion as part of wartime mobilization more generally.[2]

The polemic between French and German Catholics was only part of a much larger controversy triggered by the German invasion of Belgium in 1914. Outrage over "German atrocities" against civilians, and German counter-claims of partisan attacks, prompted a series of mutual condemnations that framed the war as a conflict about the nature and direction

---

1   Alfred Baudrillart, ed., *La Guerre Allemande et le Catholicisme* (Paris: Bloud et Gay, 1915), IX. The English translation appeared as: Alfred Baudrillart, *The German War and Catholicism* (Paris: Bloud & Gay, 1915).

2   Though the debate is not unknown, and is cited in various scholarly studies, there has been no systematic analysis of its contents thus far.

of European civilization itself.[3] This "war of words" expressed a growing sense that the war was about values as much as geography and politics, and issued in an intensely bitter controversy among intellectuals about the superiority of German *Kultur* versus Anglo-French civilization.[4] Rooted in this broader effort to "articulate an intellectual rationale for why the nation was at war," the Catholic polemic can therefore be seen as part of what Martha Hanna has dubbed the "mobilization of intellect."[5] The debate thus serves as another among the various indices for measuring how this "total" war enlisted, not just men and materiel, but ideas as well. In a related vein, one might also explain Catholic scholars' eagerness to join the war effort as part of the much broader politicization of intellectuals that Julien Benda subsequently assailed as the "treason of the intellectuals." Writing after the war, Benda accused intellectuals of betraying their traditional function as a check on the masses in favor of "the intellectual organization of political hatreds" that convinced each nation that it had a moral right to assert itself in history.[6] But as useful as these two rubrics are for understanding intellectuals' desire to join the call to arms, I want to suggest that the "mobilization of intellect" and the "treason of the intellectuals" are ultimately insufficient for understanding the Catholic polemic analyzed here. One obvious drawback of both rubrics is that they tend to suggest a uniform model of causality: in the first case, intellectuals seem almost entirely at the behest of politics; and in the second, they seem almost solely responsible for the war. But a further problem, it seems to

3   Following Horne and Kramer, I use inverted commas to distinguish the way non-Germans perceived "German atrocities" from the atrocities themselves, which though very real, should not be elided with their mythologization. See John Horne and Alan Kramer, *German Atrocities, 1914. A History of Denial* (New Haven: Yale University Press, 2001).

4   For more on the historic evolution of this debate, especially from the German side, see Fritz K. Ringer, *The Decline of the German Mandarins: The German Academic Community, 1890–1933* (Hanover: University Press of New England, 1990).

5   Martha Hanna, *The Mobilization of Intellect: French Scholars and Writers During the Great War* (Cambridge: Harvard University Press, 1996), 19.

6   Julien Benda, *The Treason of the Intellectuals*, trans., Richard Aldington (New York: Norton & Co., 1928), 27.

me, is that by lumping these Catholic polemicists together with all "intellectuals," one loses the specifically Catholic dimension of the conflict. This dimension was crucial, as I hope to show, for it provided Catholics with a distinct polemical mandate of their own, and with a means of promoting their position within the nation. By showing how the enemy was more barbaric than truly Christian—a process that I am calling a reduction to culture—Catholics used the polemic as an opportunity for challenging the popular image of Catholicism as backward by highlighting their progressive influence within the nation.

Looking at this conflict between national Churches is aimed, not at contradicting, but complimenting, the trans-national focus of much recent First World War studies. If themes like mutiny, commemoration, and revolution transcend easy classification at the national level, then religion is another manifestly trans-national phenomenon that can deepen our grasp of how war challenged Europeans' basic categories for understanding what was happening around them.[7] While it is a recognized and often lamented fact that religion did little to mitigate the slaughter of the First World War, there has been too little investigation into the distinctly religious hue the conflict had for many participants. There are important exceptions of course. In the 1970s, Albert Marrin described how the British clergy moved from seeing the conflict as a "just war" to actively promoting it as a crusade willed by God.[8] More recently, Stephan Fuchs has documented the enthusiasm of Catholic students and academics for the war.[9] Annette Becker has undertaken research into the deeply personal ways that religion shaped

7   Jay Winter, "Approaching the History of the Great War: A User's Guide," in *The Legacy of the Great War. Ninety Years On*, ed., Jay Winter (Columbia: University of Missouri Press, 2010).

8   Albert Marrin, *The Last Crusade. The Church of England in the First World War* (Durham: Duke University Press, 1974). For similar studies on Protestant clergy, see Charles E. Bailey, "The British Protestant Theologians in the First World War: Germanophobia Unleashed," in *The Harvard Theological Review* 77:2 (1984); and Frank J. Gordon, "Liberal German Churchmen and the First World War," in *German Studies Review* 4 (1981).

9   Stephan Fuchs, *"Vom Segen des Krieges": Katholische Gebildete im Ersten Weltkrieg. Eine Studie zur Kriegsdeutung im akademischen Katholizismus* (Stuttgart: Franz Steiner Verlag, 2004).

experience in wartime and postwar France.[10] And Keith Jenkins has argued that the war was viewed as a "day and night struggle against cosmic evil," and shown how in a variety of instances "the war created a spiritual excitement that burst the bounds of conventional religion."[11]

But while these and other studies have contributed immensely to our understanding of how religious people reacted to the war, they have tended to affirm a rather traditional view of religion, that is to say, as either a quasi-irrational impulse towards violence (in the form of the crusade) or as comfort in hard times.[12] This essay explores how religion—in this instance Catholicism—played a much more complex role than is generally recognized.[13] By exploring the stakes involved in the distinctly Catholic interpretation of events, it moves beyond looking at religion as a "framework of meaning," that is to say, a more or less protean set of "beliefs" that structure how people think and feel.[14] In so doing, it establishes a different perspective for understanding how the war constituted a new set of circumstances for religion to refashion itself.

10 Annette Becker, *War and Faith: The Religious Imagination in France, 1914–1930* (New York: Berg, 1998).

11 Keith Jenkins, *The Great and Holy War* (New York: Harper Collins, 2014), 10.

12 For a critique of these and other similar approaches, see José Casanova, *Public Religions in the Modern World* (Chicago: University of Chicago Press, 1994); and Hans Joas, *Do We Need Religion?*

13 In looking more deeply at religion, I am following Annette Becker, whose analysis of the deeply spiritual ties binding battle lines and home front is very compelling. Similarly, her more general argument that the war called forth a "spirituality" that traversed modes of the sacred, like religion and nationalism, seems to me very much on the mark. Nevertheless, Becker's emphasis on the "consolation" religion offers is unduly narrow. Her own research into the way "[w]ar, wounds, death [and] the supposedly temporary separation from loved ones ... created new and more intense spiritual needs" actually suggests that religion was doing much more than simply consoling people. See Becker, *War and Faith: The Religious Imagination in France, 1914–1930*, 4; and Annette Becker, "Faith Ideologies, and the 'Cultures of War'," in *A Companion to the First World War*, ed., John Horne (Malden, MA: Wiley-Blackwell, 2010).

14 This is the phrase Horne and Kramer use to describe socialists and Catholics, but it serves well to denote the typical way cultural historians approach religion. See Horne and Kramer, *German Atrocities, 1914. A History of Denial*, 262.

The French Attack

Like so many books circulating at the time, *The German War and Culture* was a response to the violation of Belgian neutrality and expressed outrage at "German atrocities" in occupied Belgium and France. Not surprisingly, the book extolled the virtues of French soldiers and especially the French clergy, whose battlefield ministry ensured that soldiers' conduct always conformed to the "Christian laws of war." It also paid appropriate homage to France's special role in world Catholicism and Christian civilization more generally. As one anonymous contributor asked: "Would not the cause of Christian civilization and of Catholicism fail ... with the disappearance of France, with the annihilation of its material and moral means?"[15] The book's main thrust, however, was to show how the war was merely the latest phase of a much larger campaign to assert "German" dominance—a campaign that had distinctly pagan roots. As Baudrillart put it in his Foreword: "Let's see whether, in the doctrine of its intellectuals, in the manner it conducts war, in the acts of its commanders and soldiers, Germany doesn't comport itself, in spite of the religious declarations of its sovereign, as a theoretical and practical adversary of Catholicism, and even of Christianity altogether."[16] Though Baudrillart and other contributors paid due respect to the Catholic minority in Germany, their unremitting assault on "German" aggression placed national character ahead of this and all other mitigating circumstances.

The contributor who did most to advance this thesis was none other than Georges Goyau—historian, lecturer at the French School in Rome, and expert on the history of German Catholicism. Goyau had devoted the better part of his career to writing the history of recent German Catholicism, seeking to distill from its exceptionally tenacious battle with German Protestants lessons that might help rejuvenate the faith in France. In his *Religious Germany*, Goyau gave a detailed survey of the Catholic revival in the German territories in the nineteenth century, openly doubting whether

---

15   "La Role Catholique de la France dans le Monde," in *La Guerre Allemande et le Catholicisme*, ed., Alfred Baudrillart (Paris: Bloud et Gay, 1915), 75. The essay is signed by "un missionaire."

16   Baudrillart, ed., *La Guerre Allemande et le Catholicisme*, IX.

French Catholics could have achieved as much.[17] In *Bismarck and the Church*, he similarly paid homage to German Catholic resilience during the period of state-sponsored persecution of Catholics known as the *Kulturkampf*.[18] In *The German War and Catholicism*, Goyau extended this analysis and argued that the war was but a second phase of this same "battle for culture." If the first phase was a domestic campaign against the "spectre" of "ultramontanism," then the second constituted an imperial campaign to promote the virtues of Protestantism around the world. Both were rooted in the "systematic equation between Protestantism and Germanism," an equation that was everywhere evident in the "books of theologians, historians, and politicians … that Prussia had disseminated across Germany throughout the nineteenth century."[19] The recent construction of German Protestant churches in Rome and Jerusalem, moreover, testified in no uncertain terms to the mutually supportive role of "Protestantism" and "Germanism" in the foreign policy of the empire. Though Goyau conceded that equating Protestantism and Germanism was often a matter of politics, and conceded that it was rarely "true believers" who championed extreme nationalism, he rejected the notion that religion was merely a surface phenomenon. On the contrary, for Goyau, the underlying truth of both German politics and Protestantism was a quest for self-divination, the pursuit, namely, of a true Germanic faith. This manifested itself most clearly in Germans' sense of themselves as a nation whose destiny put them above common standards of law. But it was even plainer to see among those who, "not wanting to install any other than indigenous divinities and heralding the Germanic idea of Christianity, have moved even beyond Luther to as far as Wotan, Odin and Thor to find their authentic, indigenous, Germanic incarnation of God. Though Luther be the ideal type of German man, of the *true German* man, his Christ remained a Jew; with Wotan, one has a German God, a *true German God*."[20]

17 Georges Goyau, *L'Allemagne Religieuse: Le Catholicisme (1800–1870)* (Paris: Perrin, 1909).

18 G. Goyau, *Bismarck et l'Église: Le Culturkampf* (Paris: Perrin et cie, 1913).

19 G. Goyau, "La 'Culture' Germanique et le Catholicisme," in *La Guerre Allemande et le Catholicisme*, ed., Alfred Baudrillart (Paris: Bloud et Gay, 1915), 33.

20 Ibid., 44.

The accusation that German politics and culture were, at bottom, a re-version to barbarism is the central motif in *The German War and Catholicism*, and it is echoed throughout the various essays in the collection. Goyau's attack represents its most sustained articulation, however, and was the text most cited by German Catholics responding to the French attack. For Goyau, the danger lay in the way German culture seemed capable of justifying any and all violence:

> We are touching here upon the most practical and real conse-quences of certain philosophical speculations that, in the realm of thought, can seem but games of spirit.... But when these speculations are transported into the realm of history, becoming the games of princes and soldiers; immediately they suggest, im-mediately they glorify the most criminal atrocities.... The ad-vent of the universal Germanic idea, that is the supreme good. In the name of the Germanic idea one is authorized to do evil, as it turns necessarily to the good. One need not have extenu-ating circumstances for heinous crimes of war; philosophically, one considers them justified. Evil is in the world to give birth to the good. The German state, which according to the Hegelian philosophy is the incarnation of the moral idea ... will thus consciously and willingly make evil the object of its proper triumph.[21]

Goyau was not alone in blaming German philosophy for the war. For the Spanish-American philosopher, George Santayana, German philosophy expressed a special yearning for transcendence from mundane reality. Rooted in a rationalized Protestantism whose "beauty and torment ... is that it opens the door so wide to what lies beyond it," the unremitting de-sire to purify and overcome itself and its own inherent limits moved phi-losophy inevitably, towards "primitivism."[22] John Dewey lay the blame squarely on German idealism, declaring that "weapons forged in the

21 Ibid., 40–41.
22 George Santayana, *Egotism in German Philosophy* (New York: Haskell House Publishers, 1916).

smithy of the Absolute become brutal and cruel when confronted by merely human resistance."[23] And the American essayist William Roscoe Thayer accused all modern German philosophers "from Kant to Nietzsche" of "pull[ing] down one after another the pillars on which rested what remained of Christianity."[24] For Goyau's co-contributor, Bernard Gaudeau, German philosophy ratified "a new conception of war … more anti-Christian than one can dream."[25]

> Modern German thought suppresses the very notion of justice and morality, for the moral law is nothing if it is not objective and absolute, and German thought admits of nothing that is objective and absolute…. Religiously since Luther, rationally and philosophically since Kant and Hegel, nationally since Fichte, militarily since Bismarck (and all of the terms of this progression present themselves according to the most impeccable logic), the German "I" recognizes nothing beneath itself in the world; no objective rule, neither religious, moral, nor legal.[26]

For all these critics, German nationalism was underwritten by a philosophy capable of justifying every atrocity in the name of self-advancement. War in the trenches was thus the outgrowth of deeply rooted spiritual differences, that is to say, culture, and not politics.

The German Rejoinder

Given its thesis, one wonders why it was German Catholics and not Protestants who took the lead in responding to the book. Nevertheless, in 1915, the "Standing Committee on Catholics in Public Life" published *The*

---

23 John Dewey, *German Philosophy and Politics* (New York: Henry Holt, 1916), 43.

24 William Roscoe Thayer, *Germany vs. Civilization. Notes on the Atrocious War* (Boston: Houghton Mifflin, 1916), 62.

25 Bernard Gaudeau, "Les Lois Chrétiennes de la Guerre," in *La Guerre Allemande et le Catholicisme*, ed. Alfred Baudrillart (Paris: Bloud et Gay, 1915), 24–25.

26 Ibid.

German War and Catholicism: A German Defense Against French Attacks.[27] In it, they denied that Germany was guilty of starting the war or of committing atrocities, and decried the effort to make this a "religious war." Not surprisingly, the authors were especially determined to deflect the charge that Germany was fundamentally Protestant, and that there was anything pagan lurking in German politics or culture. But what is especially noteworthy is less their repeated affirmation that Germans were overwhelmingly "good Christians" who had absolutely no desire to worship Wotan, than their determined effort to turn the tables and accuse the French of the most corrosive anti-Christian tendencies. Indeed, they attacked Goyau's claim that the war was an outgrowth of the *Kulturkampf*, and charged the French with nurturing the heresy recently dubbed "Modernism":

> It is a sick passion that seeks to trace everything that is evil and wrong in France to origins in Germany. That one can find seeds of Modernism in Kant is true, but why did one allow Modernism to fester [in France] while, at the same time, German Catholics remained largely untouched by it? But when it is said that Prince Bismarck transferred the fight against the Church to France—that is absurd. Culture war is not an export item.[28]

According to German Catholics, France was the true enemy of Catholicism; for it was there that religion had been extirpated from public life to the greatest degree. In view of the comprehensive "laicization" of French society that had occurred in the previous decade, as a result of the 1905 law separating church and state, German Catholics charged that the majority of children in France were "growing up without God."[29] Citing the long history of anti-clericalism

27 *Der deutsche Krieg und der Katholizismus: Deutsche Abwehr französischer Angriffe. Herausgegeben von deutschen Katholiken* (Berlin: Germania, 1915).

28 Ibid., 92. Condemned in 1907 by Pius X in his encyclical *Pascendi Dominici gregis*, modernism is less a definite theological error than a loose collection of attempts to adapt Catholicism to the intellectual trends of the time. See Alec R. Vidler, *A Variety of Catholic Modernists* (London: Cambridge University Press, 1970).

29 Growing out of a post-Dreyfus campaign against the Church, the "laicization" of France consisted in a campaign to expel religious orders, a repudiation of

and anti-Catholicism in France since the revolution, they declared that the French were in no position to accuse Germans of a reversion to barbarism. After all, their behavior in the present conflict was hardly above reproach. Looking at France's multi-ethnic allies—and with no small amount of racism—the Germans asked: "And so is it those who fight alongside Turks, Senegalese, Arabs, Hindus, Gurkhas, Sikhs, Kyrgyzstanis, Tatars, Chechens, Kalmucks, and Turkmenestanis who fight for true culture and civilization?"[30]

The effort to unmask the French as barbarians was even more pronounced in the larger collection of essays titled *German Culture, Catholicism, and the World War* published in 1916.[31] Edited by George Pfeilschrifter, Professor of Theology at the University of Freiburg, it consisted of essays refuting the French charges in more depth and traversed such topics as: "The Justice and Necessity of the World War," "Belgium's Neutrality and Its Doom," "The Care of Religious Souls and Religious Life in the German Army," "The Psychology of Atrocity Reports," "Art and Sacred Buildings in the War," and "German and French War-Pastorals." Central to the book, however, were a series of essays aimed at refuting the attack against German culture. In his "The Declaration of Literary Warfare by the French Catholics," Professor of Moral Theology at the University of Münster, Joseph Mausbach, railed against the attempt to "interpret German misdeeds—philosophically, as it were—as a *system* of barbarism." He denied furthermore that the "sins of individuals" could be attributed to the "barbarism and godlessness of the German people as a whole."[32] In his essay,

the Concordat, and a wholesale set of restrictions on the role of religion in public life. For more detail, see Nicholas Atkin and Frank Tellet, *Priests, Prelates and People: A History of European Catholicism since 1750* (Oxford: Oxford University Press, 2003).

30 *Der deutsche Krieg und der Katholizismus: Deutsche Abwehr französischer Angriffe. Herausgegeben von deutschen Katholiken*, 81.

31 Georg Pfeilschifter, ed., *Deutsche Kultur, Katholizismus, und Weltkrieg. Eine Abwehr des Buches "Le Guerre Allemande et le Catholicisme"* (Freiburg im Breisgau: Herder, 1916). The English translation appeared as Georg Pfeilschifter, ed., *German Culture, Catholicism, and the World War: A Defense Against the Book* La Guerre Allemande et le Catholicisme (St. Paul: Wanderer Printing Co., 1916).

32 Joseph Mausbach, "The Declaration of Literary Warfare by French Catholics," in *German Culture, Catholicism and the World War*, ed., Georg Pfeilschifter (St. Paul: Wanderer Printing Co., 1916), 23.

"The French and the German *Kulturkampf* in their Causes and Effects," Hermann Platz returned to the issue of French radicalism:

> The German *Kulturkampf* is an isolated episode without an historical prologue or epilogue; the French *Kulturkampf* is a systematic unfolding of a basic plan drawn up already during the period of the French Revolution and ever since kept more or less clearly in view. The German *Kulturkampf* is anti-Catholic; the French deeply anti-Christian and anti-religious.[33]

Similarly, the Bonn historian Heinrich Schrörs, though conceding that "in Germany, there has been a philosophy of pantheism," dismissed as a "monstrous exaggeration" that this was "the foundation of present German 'culture'."[34] Once again, what is striking is not the denials themselves, but the parallel attempt to unmask France as the origin of a particularly modern, secular—and so ultimately anti-Christian—turn of mind. Schrörs, for one, declared:

> On our part, we could ... present a counter bill, which would not only have its full value, but leave a balance in our favor. As Germany has its pantheism, so France has its positivism ... [which] fills the heads of the state school teachers who set the tone in the communes. It constitutes not only a philosophical school, but rather a sect. This positivism is atheistic. God, spirit, human personality as a substantial soul, are subjective imaginations without objective reality. Morality without God, and the school without religion, are the products of positivism. Its purposes, which it accomplished only too well, were to transform the nation into a society without God and king, and to establish firmly the republic and a "lay spirit."

33 Hermann Platz, "The French and the German Kulturkampf in their Causes and Effects," in *German Culture, Catholicism and the World War*, ed., Georg Pfeilschifter (St. Paul: Wanderer Printing Co., 1916), 258.

34 Heinrich Schrörs, "Is the War a War of Religion?" in *German Culture, Catholicism and the World War*, ed., Georg Pfeilschifter (St. Paul: Wanderer Printing Co., 1916), 65.

Though Schrörs assured readers that he was not, in fact, "mak[ing] this assertion," and was only suggesting he could make it, he left no doubt that "if the war on the part of France is produced by its culture, then it is a war for atheistic naturalism."[35] In a similar disavowal, Mausbach solemnly promised that "German Catholics will never ... attribute to their opponents ... the motive of moral barbarism and religious hatred in the way in which the authors of this book have attributed it to Germany."[36] Still, though denying that this was their intention, both men made these accusations all the same.

Intellectuals and the Reduction to Culture

By seeking to defeat the enemy's values, Catholic polemicists joined other intellectuals in reducing complex political, military, and economic realities to allegedly pre-reflective traits deeply embedded in, and so definitive of, national culture. The formula for this reduction was evident even before the war. In his 1913 lectures on "Germany and England," the Scottish historian John Adam Cramb analyzed the looming conflict between the two powers, and declared Germany's status as a relative latecomer to be the result of having repressed its own native "world-vision" for too long. Having adopted the religion of Rome, "she has struggled and wrestled to see with eyes that were not her eyes, to worship a God that was not her God, to live with a world-vision that was not her vision."[37] Having finally liberated "her own genius for religion," however, German philosophy had restored "German imagination back [to] where it was with Alaric and Theodoric."[38] During the war, the reduction to culture took on added meaning. Seeking to clarify Allied accusations of German "barbarism," the Danish author, Jacob Peter Bang, paid due respect to the unquestionable achievements of German science

35 Ibid., 66.
36 Mausbach, "The Declaration of Literary Warfare by French Catholics," op. cit., 14.
37 John Adam Cramb, *Germany and England* (New York: E. P. Dutton & Co., 1915), 127.
38 Ibid., 129.

and literature, but declared that "the charge of barbarism points in an entirely different direction."[39] The real issue was the evolution, in recent decades, of a distinctly German "craving for power" and "worship of mere strength" at the expense of any regard for international law.[40] Pointing to a "certain hardness" and "cynical brutality," Bang judged "the most characteristic trait of Germanism" to be the unquestioned belief that "their actions rest upon a moral basis" and that "the German people as such cannot possibly be wrong." The reduction to culture could be used in a variety of ways, depending on the circumstances. If some saw the ultimate bedrock of values as philosophical or religious, others saw it as biological. In his assessment of German "atavism," William Roscoe Thayer observed how "[o]ne of those traits, blood-thirstiness, crops out at intervals during all their subsequent annals, as surely as periodic dipsomania recurs to madden its victim."[41] And in his account of the time he spent in Belgium at German Headquarters as a relief worker, the American biologist Vernon Kellogg described how German officers uniformly viewed the conflict in strictly Darwinian terms as a struggle for the survival of the fittest.[42] Whatever the angle, critics were united in their desire to unmask high-blown theory as crass cover for base motives, and document the hypocrisy of German pretensions to fighting in the name of *Kultur*.[43]

Used negatively, the reduction to culture aimed to expose the barbarity

---

39 Jacob Peter Bang, *Hurrah and Hallelujah. The Teaching of Germany's Poets, Prophets, Professors and Preachers. A Documentation*, trans., Ralph Connor (New York: George H. Doran Company, 1917), 17.

40 Ibid., 22.

41 Thayer, *Germany vs. Civilization. Notes on the Atrocious War*, op. cit., 25.

42 Vernon Kellogg, *Headquarters Nights. A Record of Conversations and Experiences at the Headquarters of the German Army in France and Belgium* (Boston: The Atlantic Monthly Press, 1917). For an interesting discussion of how this self-conscious Darwinian justification for conflict influenced William Jennings Bryan, see Edward B. Davis, "Fundamentalists Cartoons, Modernist Pamphlets, and the Religious Image of Science in the Scopes Era," in *Religion and the Culture of Print in Modern America*, ed., Charles L. Cohen and Paul S. Boyer (Madison: University of Wisconsin Press, 2008).

43 Joseph Bédier, *Les crimes allemands d'après des témoignages allemands* (Paris: Armand Colin, 1915), 39.

of the enemy. But it could be used positively as well, that is, to explain one's superiority. This was the case with the famous "Address to the World of Culture," published in 1914 after the outbreak of war.[44] Signed by ninety-three prominent German scholars, the "Manifesto of the 93," as it was also called, denied that Germany had wanted war, violated Belgian neutrality, or committed any atrocities. It maligned the enemy as "purported defenders of European civilization, who united with Russians and Serbs in order to treat the world to a shameful play, inciting Mongols and Negroes against the white race."[45] And it celebrated the unmitigated superiority of German culture. It also declared that "[w]ithout German militarism, German culture would have long ago been destroyed. It has emerged from it in order to defend it in a land that has for hundreds of years been plagued by roving bandits like no other."[46] Though a number of the signatories later disavowed knowing its precise contents before signing it, the "Manifesto" was no less paradigmatic of the reduction to culture.[47] By making culture the generative matrix for everything else, it set the terms for so much of the wartime debate.

In the midst of the larger "war of words," the reduction to culture cut through sterile academic theorizing to the alleged vital core of national differences. For many intellectuals, as Roland Stromberg points out, this affirmation of a kind of fundamental "irrationalism" channeled a "destructive joy of rebelling against a sterile culture." In stark contrast to the elevating pretensions of so much discourse about culture or civilization, the reduction to culture meant "affirming the individual's right to realize himself" and "yearning to re-create the primitive community where art and instinct

44 By choosing to translate "An die Kulturwelt" as "Address to the World of Culture," I depart from those who translate it as "Address to the Civilized World." Given that the "Address" itself was aimed at shoring up the classic distinction of German *Kultur* vs. "civilization," it seems eminently preferable to maintain the spirit of this goal when translating the title. For a detailed analysis of the history surrounding the document, and foreign reactions, see Juergen von Ungern-Sternberg and Wolfgang von Ungern-Sternberg, *Der Aufruf 'An die Kulturwelt.' Das Manifest der 93 und die Anfaenge der Kriegspropaganda im Ersten Weltkrieg* (Stuttgart: Franz Steiner Verlag, 1996).

45 "An die Kulturwelt," in *Berliner Tageblatt*, October 4, 1914.

46 Ibid.

47 George Renwick, "Kultur Manifesto Foisted on Signers," in *New York Times*, November 5 1920.

rule."[48] For the American, Randolph Bourne, it was a significant step away from higher ideals that no longer rang true:

> It is not so much what they thought as how they felt that explains our intellectual class. Allowing for colonial sympathy, there was still the personal shock in a world-war which outraged all our pre-conceived notions of the way the world was tending. It reduced to rubbish most of the humanitarian internationalism and democratic nationalism which had been the emotional thread of our intellectuals' life.[49]

Bourne saw everywhere a "reversion ... to more primitive ways of thinking," including a preference for "simple syllogisms," "labels," and calls for "direct action" at all costs. Inverting the normal assumption about how people should act according to their values, the war transcended easy classification and revealed the certainties of civilization to be much more transient and even arbitrary than previously thought. In this context, where unprecedented carnage created a need for new categories to describe experience, intellectuals sought firmer ground in the imagined bedrock of national culture.[50]

What explains this triumph of national chauvinism over cosmopolitanism? There is, and probably never can be a definitive answer. For many, the war no doubt offered a means of transcending mundane "bourgeois" materialist values.[51] For scholars, artists, writers—whose stock in trade was

48 Roland Stromberg, *Redemption by War: The Intellectuals and 1914* (Lawrence: The Regents Press of Kansas, 1982), 10.

49 Randolph Bourne, "The War and the Intellectuals," in *Untimely Papers* (New York: W. Huebsch, 1919), 35. The essay itself was originally published in June 1917.

50 For a stimulating argument about how the war was the crucible for a distinctly modernist sensibility, see Modris Eksteins, *Rites of Spring. The Great War and the Birth of the Modern Age* (New York: Anchor Books, 1989).

51 Wolfgang J. Mommsen, "German Artists, Writers and Intellectuals and the Meaning of War, 1914–18," in *State, Society, and Mobilization in Europe during the First World War*, ed., John Horne (London: Cambridge University Press, 2001).

working in the medium of mind or "spirit"—the call to arms was an opportunity to reassert the role of deeper and more important values, like
courage, sacrifice, and even creativity. Many believed that destruction would
clear the way for new acts of creation. This was clearly the case for the historian Otto von Gierke, who declared that "the mightiest of culture-de-
stroyers is, at the same time, the mightiest forger of culture."[52] Others, like
Stromberg, have argued that the deeper impulse towards national chauvinism lay in a kind of rush to community. In view of their negative assessment
of the sterility of bourgeois materialism and the atomization of society, intellectuals were predisposed to see the war as a means to restoring true
bonds of community.[53] Whatever the reason, one dimension of the "war
of words" that should be stressed is how it pushed intellectuals to rescind
membership in what might be termed the "imagined community" of universalist and rationalist discourse.[54] Forged in the Enlightenment, on the
model of a republic of letters, this community was always an important
counterbalance to the centripetal force of nationalism during the nineteenth
century. With the outbreak of the First World War, however, this imagined
community suffered a withering blow. Indeed, one way of understanding
the reduction to barbarism is to see it as the inverse of what Ian Hunter
has called the "spiritual exercises" that helped establish the "truth-capable
subject" during the Enlightenment. Aimed at promoting "pure intellec-
tion," these exercises consisted in disciplined efforts to overcome confused
empirical sensations to forge the "comportment-ideal of a prestigious way
of life, that of the secular sage."[55] Transcending local and mundane attach-
ments, such sages constituted an international fraternity of scholars and intellectuals capable of relating to one another on the plane of pure ideas

52 Otto von Gierke, "Krieg und Kultur," in *Deutsche Reden in Schwerer Zeit, ed.
    Zentralstelle für Volkswollfahrt* (Berlin: Heymanns, 1914), 81.
53 Stromberg, *Redemption by War: The Intellectuals and 1914.*
54 As an equally distinct product of print culture, this "imagined community"
    of universalist discourse should be seen as structurally paired with nationalism
    as Benedict Anderson has analyzed it. See Benedict Anderson, *Imagined Com-
    munities: Reflections on the Origin and Spread of Nationalism* (New York: Verso,
    1983).
55 Ian Hunter, *Rival Enlightenments: Civil and Metaphysical Philosophy in Early
    Modern Germany* (New York: Cambridge University Press, 2001), 104.

unencumbered from petty national entanglements. By contrast, the reduction to culture and mutual accusations of barbarism sought to restore the "truth-capable subject" to its national roots, shattering this ideal plane undergirding international professional relationships.[56]

Like socialists and other "international communities of truth," Catholics maintained "a genuine belief ... that the meaning of the war could be judged by some absolute truth."[57] Nevertheless, they were generally critical of the Enlightenment already, and therefore suffered no great sense of loss at the implosion of the imagined community of universalist discourse.[58] Instead, their frustration stemmed more from Pope Benedict XV's resolve to remain impartial during the course of the war. The Pope's refusal to take sides was especially difficult in view of the fact that Catholics were used to appealing to Rome for definitive answers. But with too many Catholics on both sides of the lines, the Pope castigated war itself as evil, and resisted condemning any one nation.[59] A consummate diplomat, Benedict XV made several efforts at negotiating an end to hostilities. But his desire to remain neutral prompted some, including the apostate French theologian Alfred Loisy, to accuse the pope of abrogating his moral duty to condemn evil deeds wherever and whenever they occurred. Condemned in 1908 for his "Modernist" approach to biblical interpretation, Loisy attacked Benedict XV's consistorial allocution of January 1915, calling it an intervention by "one who has spoken only for the express purpose of saying nothing." Where the pope "should have proclaimed the eternal disgrace of a civilization which ended in this butchery," in no uncertain terms and without distinction, his "vague lament over the misfortune of war" betrayed the singular fact that the pope was not a "representative of humanity," but

56 Romain Roland was among the few who laments the deeply negative effects of nationalism and the war on European networks of scholarly cooperation and exchange. Romain Rolland, *I Will Not Rest*, trans., by K. S. Shelvankar (London: Liverlight Press, 1937).

57 Horne and Kramer, *German Atrocities, 1914: A History of Denial*, 262.

58 Harm Kleuting, *Katholische Aufklärung, Aufklärung im katholischen Deutschland* (Hamburg: Meiner Verlag, 1993).

59 For a good biography of Benedict XV, see John F. Pollard, *The Unknown Pope: Benedict XV (1914–1922) and the Pursuit of Peace* (London: Geoffrey Chapman, 1999).

a "government functionary" and the "administrator of an ancient ecclesiastical creed and organization."[60] In the end, Loisy doubted that Christians would ever overcome their national hatreds.[61] Such hatreds, after all, were not a temporary anomaly caused by the war, but were rooted in Christianity's historical evolution:

> From the first, [Christianity] offered itself rather as an international contrafraternity than an universal religion: it became the religion of the Roman Empire; and, from this imperial religion, there descended, in varying forms, Roman Catholicism, the national churches of the East, and the reformed communities. One can see why the present crisis, with the anguish it causes and the questions it intensifies, seems to break through the ancient creeds, and the explanations they give, and the promises they make.[62]

Christianity was incapable of transcending the national hatreds fueling the conflict. According to Loisy, therefore, the only real hope lay in the possibility that the war might precipitate the collapse of the Churches. Only then might it be possible to evolve "the super-religion, which our crucified humanity is bringing to birth through so many dolours."

Loisy's attack on the pope helps put into focus what other Catholics might have been feeling, but were too afraid to say.[63] Though perhaps overly harsh, his indictment of the papacy points to an important structural feature of the modern Catholic Church, one that helps us better understand both the pope's position and the debate between French and German Catholics. In contrast with its forceful and stated opposition to change and accommodation to the modern world, the Catholic Church had actually undergone a dramatic shift in its self-understanding over the course of the

60 Alfred Firmin Loisy, *The War and Religion*, trans., Arthur Galton (Oxford: Blackwell, 1915), 42–50.
61 Ibid., x.
62 Ibid., 76.
63 For a brief overview of the pope's attempts to maintain Catholic unity in the face of this frustration, see Horne and Kramer, *German Atrocities, 1914. A History of Denial.*

nineteenth century.[64] In view of the steady erosion of its sovereign power, beginning with the French Revolution and culminating in the loss of the Papal States in 1870, the Church had recast itself as an institution based on popular support to a new and unprecedented degree.[65] Accompanied by a popular Catholic revival, this shift saw the pope retreat from his historic role as a sovereign prince to emerge as an increasingly dominant influence in the everyday lives of Catholics.[66] And in the context of the First World War, this does much to explain both Benedict XV's decision to stay neutral (wanting not to alienate any national group) and Catholics' frustration with the absence of moral leadership (they had come to expect papal condemnations of the "evils" of the modern world).[67] By refusing to take sides, he left a vacuum in which national Church initiatives came to the fore. In this situation, the polemic between French and German Catholics can be seen as a paradoxical attempt to define the right "Catholic" response in national, rather than "universal," terms.

Overcoming Backwardness

In view of the destruction of the cathedral at Rheims and attacks on Catholic clergy, the vaunted German claim to represent deeper spiritual values embodied in the idea of *Kultur* struck many European Catholics, in particular, as hollow indeed. As Annette Becker shows, French Catholics concluded that such atrocities "were not the acts of a civilized nation," but "proved that the Germans were a race of barbarians, situated somewhere between the Mongols and the Vandals, and of whom Martin Luther was both descendant and symbol."[68] Calling Germans barbarians amounted to

---

64 Vincent Viaene, "The Roman Question, Catholic Mobilisation and Papal Diplomacy," in *The Black International*, ed., Emiel Lamberts (Brussels: Brepols, 2002).

65 Atkin and Tellet, *Priests, Prelates and People: A History of European Catholicism since 1750*; and Owen Chadwick, *The Popes and European Revolution* (Oxford: Oxford University Press, 1981).

66 Gene Burns, *The Frontiers of Catholicism: The Politics of Ideology in a Liberal World*.

67 Horne and Kramer, *German Atrocities, 1914: A History of Denial.*

68 Becker, *War and Faith: The Religious Imagination in France, 1914–1930*, 11.

more than mud-slinging however. Showing one's enemy to be barbaric effectively reinforced a view of all "culture" as ultimately national, and this set the stage for French and German Catholics to reassert their own relevance to national culture in a way that helped them shore up their profile within the nation. If French Catholics could portray German Protestantism as ultimately akin to a desire for a return to Wotan, then it only strengthened them in their claim that something deep in the French nation helped nurture a better kind of Catholicism, and that France was the favored daughter of the Church.[69] By the same token, if Germans could portray Modernism as an offshoot of positivism and the anti-Christian impulses of the French Revolution, then it likewise strengthened the claim that something deep in the German nation helped produce a better kind of Catholicism, such as might be found in German contributions to neoscholasticism. For both groups of Catholics, the reduction to culture legitimized the nation as the basic frame of reference in ways that had important ramifications. For it meant that the path of each nation from barbarism to Christian civilization could be compared and contrasted to good effect. That French and German Catholics seized on this comparison to strengthen their domestic image, as we shall see, helps explain their unique and significant bid to mobilize under distinctly Catholic auspices.

Both French and German Catholics had reasons for demonstrating their loyalty in a time of war, and yet it would be incorrect to see their mobilization as merely a case of subordinating faith to the nation.[70] On the contrary, their polemic shows how defending the faith in the name of the nation was not a simple process but rooted in a distinct experience of being Catholic at the beginning of the twentieth century. Like feminists and socialists, Catholics seized the opportunity provided by the war to burnish their credentials as true patriots.[71] As Stephan Fuchs has shown, German Catholics reconciled their faith with the cause of the nation by seeing the

---

69 Citing the prayer of Joan of Arc, Gaudeau states: "To fight against France is to fight against God." See Gaudeau, "Les Lois Chrétiennes de la Guerre," 30.

70 Christopher Dowe, *Auch Bildungsbürger. Katholische Studierende und Akademiker im Kaiserreich* (Göttingen: Vandenhoeck & Ruprecht, 2005).

71 Jo Vellacott, "Feminist Consciousness and the First World War," in *History Workshop Journal* 23 (1987).

war as a divinely ordained test. And their conviction that French Catholics were lapsed, indifferent, and generally "bad" Catholics reassured them that they were passing God's test by slaughtering their co-religionists.[72] But why accuse each other of a reversion to barbarity? Why not rest content with simply accusing the other of sinfulness or untrammeled nationalism? To answer this, one must look at what both sides claimed as their unique advantage as "French" and "German" Catholics, and how this stands out against the background created by an image of a reversion to barbarity. And this requires taking account of how both sides framed their attacks against the background of prior secular-Catholic/Protestant-Catholic conflicts.

For French Catholics, of course, the new prohibitions on religion's public presence, comprehensively known as *laïcité*, were an affront to a deeply felt connection between Catholicism and French identity. That this wasn't the first time such a connection had been severed in the name of republicanism must have only heightened the desire to overcome or transcend this division by any means possible. It is significant therefore that the French attack against German barbarism served as the means for a resolutely Catholic appraisal of the fundamentally sacred character of the nation; an appraisal that sought to overcome the shallowness of republicanism and lay bare what must be a deeper bond between the individual and the nation. This emerged particularly clearly in Gaudeau's "The Christian Laws of War," in which he contrasted the secular civil code with "Catholic morality." Since war suspended the civil code, Gaudeau argued that it was essential to let Catholic morality guide the individual in his comportment, for such morality "fixes objective, absolute, and immutable laws that neither emanate from nor are dependent on individual conscience." Moral principles were not identifiable with the "national conscience on which they are imposed," but constituted "God's will … freely revealed, known by human reason as part of the natural order, and by Christian revelation."[73] Of course, Catholic morality dictated that one not harm non-combatants, and that one carry out one's battlefield duties without malice. But war itself, though perhaps deplorable, was as much a part of the order of things as Christian charity.

---

72 Fuchs, *"Vom Segen des Krieges": Katholische Gebildete im Ersten Weltkrieg. Eine Studie zur Kriegsdeutung im akademischen Katholizismus*, 226.
73 Gaudeau, "Les Lois Chrétiennes de la Guerre," 3.

Citing the Gospels of Matthew and Luke, Gaudeau held that the nation had a pride of place in God's order. Therefore,

> [i]n this order of charity, in this hierarchy of objects towards which we carry our love … our fatherland takes pride of place. We touch here on the foundation of the theology of patriotism, which is too little understood, and about which I will elaborate, for the principle of our duty towards the fatherland is also one of the Christian laws of war.[74]

Gaudeau's theology of patriotism was rooted in the inescapable fact that humans were indebted to God, family, and country for their very existence. As such, it followed that individuals owed each "debtor" respect, obedience, and love. "Without God, we would not exist; without our family and our country, we would not be who we are." The upshot of this was not only that family and country should be seen as more or less equivalent, but that duty to the nation took precedence over duty to the rest of humanity: "And since our fatherland is nothing but the normal and historical development of the family, our duties toward the fatherland are an extension of our duties towards our family, as stated in God's fourth commandment. We do not owe the same pious worship to the rest of humanity as to our family and our fatherland, because the rest of humanity has no similar claim on us.…"[75]

Whether or not this accurately reflects Thomistic teaching on "patriotic piety," as Gaudeau claimed, I cannot say. Nor do I have much to say in this context about Gaudeau's claim that this did not justify conquest but only defense of one's country. The point that needs to be made here is that this sacralization of the nation was a clear bid by French Catholics to reclaim relevance in a France refashioned according to the principles of *laïcité*. Accusing the Germans of barbarism was thus not only mud-slinging or war-mongering, but served to make more plausible the idea that French Catholicism could be a contemporary and effective resource in the nation's ideological arsenal at a time of crisis. Having been forced to take a back

74 Ibid., 6.
75 Ibid., 8.

seat by a republicanism that fashioned itself as modern, progressive, and secular, the real task for French Catholics was to prove that they had something to offer. In this context, accusing Germans of barbarism helped defuse the charge, common since the Enlightenment, that Catholicism was itself simply an atavistic hold-over of the Middle Ages.[76] By revealing Germans to be barbaric and hence backward, French Catholics re-cast themselves and their faith as a decidedly contemporary resource in French culture that could be mobilized to a good end, namely in the moral justification of the conflict. That this would catapult French Catholics ahead of republicanism in the French political imagination was, of course, too much to hope for; but scoring a blow against Protestantism, Kant, and the Kaiser was aimed as much at restoring Catholicism to a legitimate place in French "culture" as it was in reducing German culture to barbarism.

What about German Catholics? Like their French counterparts, they too seized the advantage provided by reducing the enemy to barbarity as a foil against which to secure advantages for themselves in a larger battle for culture. But here of course the goal was not to arrive at a point at or near secular republicanism, but to find a way to pull ahead in the competition between an allegedly backward Catholicism and an allegedly progressive Protestantism.[77] This competition, which plagued German history in various forms throughout the nineteenth century, came to a head in the years following the founding of the second German Empire, when Bismarck launched his famous "*Kulturkampf*" against Catholics.[78] And it was given a decidedly new impetus at the turn of the century when new statistical information revealed that Catholics lagged behind Protestants in education

---

76 Atkin and Tellet, *Priests, Prelates and People: A History of European Catholicism since 1750*, op. cit.

77 Helmut Walser Smith, *German Nationalism and Religious Conflict: Culture, Ideology, Politics, 1870–1914* (Princeton, N.J.: Princeton University Press, 1995).

78 Translating, literally, as "war for culture," the *Kulturkampf* consisted of a series of laws and restrictions directed against Catholics between 1872 and 1878. Michael B. Gross, *The War Against Catholicism: Liberalism and the Anti-Catholic Imagination in Nineteenth-Century Germany* (University of Michigan Press, 2004).

and good jobs.[79] Fearing the long-term implications of Catholic backwardness, one Munich newspaper painted the following picture:

> In spite of their protests, Catholics will be gradually yet systematically pushed out of the more important and influential positions of intellectual and economic life of the nation. First they will grow poorer, and following that, will be increasingly less able to send their children into higher education. The existing disparity will only grow wider until nothing further can help, since the means themselves are lacking.[80]

A desire to refute and overcome this image helps us understand why German Catholics might use the image of a progressive Germany surrounded by barbarians as a way of helping propel themselves out of their backwardness, even if this meant conceding the forward momentum of Protestantism. Thus the Regensburger Deacon, Franz Xaver Kiefl, accused Goyau and his cohort of having overlooked the real implications of a progressive Protestantism. Progress in recent decades had indeed precipitated "an internal crisis ... [that] actually produced an irenical effect on inter-denominational relations" according to Kiefl. For precisely to the extent that liberal theologians after Schleiermacher had initiated a progressive dilution of the old Lutheran orthodoxy, many Protestants now found themselves closer to the Catholic position in their desire to defend the status quo from innovation. Equally beneficial, as Kiefl saw it, was the fact that the more radical strands of liberal theology had "relinquished a multitude of dogmatic and historical prejudices against the Catholic Church."[81] Though he was quick to downplay any possibility

---

79 The debate was provoked by statistics appearing in Georg Mayr's *Allgemeines Statistisches Archiv*, and was formative in the evolution of Weber's *Protestant Ethic and the Spirit of Capitalism*.

80 This is from an article in the *Münchener Neuesten Nachrichten* (no. 167) and is quoted in: Herman Schell, *Der Katholicismus als Princip des Fortschritts* (Würzburg: Andreas Göbel, 1897), 5.

81 Francis Xavier Kiefl, "Catholicism and Protestantism in Modern Germany," in *German Culture, Catholicism and World War*, ed., Georg Pfeilschifter (St. Paul: Wanderer Printing Co., 1916), 285.

of imminent reunion between the confessions, Kiefl concluded that "Catholicism and Protestantism in Germany are today, more than ever before, bound to cooperate in the common defense of the fundamental truths of Christianity."[82] What makes this conclusion so interesting in the context of the polemic against French Catholics is that it paints a picture of a necessary historical *Aufhebung*: a historical "transformation of Protestantism ... [that] of necessity brought about a decided change in the evaluation of Catholicism." As much as Catholics in Germany might fear their backwardness *vis a vis* German Protestants, they had less to fear if they conceived of themselves as locked in a mutually provocative historical advance whose outcome was a "common defense of the fundamental truths of Christianity."

Conclusion

In the end, only a relatively small number of Christians were able to transcend wartime hostilities to advocate peace during the Great War. This fact makes it essential to understand just how Christians, and in this instance Catholics, put their faith in service of the conflict. It is not enough to observe with sad or wistful irony how religion succumbed to nationalism—or fascism, or communism in later years—as though this were somehow predestined to happen. For it can lead us to see religion too uniformly as a victim of these forces, and prevent us from asking just how religion perhaps enabled, encouraged, or made common cause with them. If the polemic between French and German Catholics tells us anything, it is that Catholics were both willing and able to use Catholicism itself as a platform for hostile attacks against their enemies. It also shows how Catholics were eager to turn the situation to their own advantage, and sought to defray prevailing images of Catholicism as backwards and anti-modern. This does not mean that Catholics were any more or less disposed towards propaganda and polemics. But in taking up the cause of the nation, Catholics did so as Catholics, without necessarily doubting their ability to be good Germans and good French as well.

John Horne makes the important point that wartime mobilization involved harnessing collective imagination as much as the power of the

82   Ibid., 293.

state.[83] From this perspective, it is especially important to avoid treating religion as merely serving as the background to action, supplying meaning in the form of values, beliefs, or consolation in times of crisis, and so reducing it to culture. Given the radically changing circumstances ushered in by the war, it makes more sense to consider the ways that religion itself was subject to reconstruction in unpredictable ways. For religion to mean anything, it had to keep pace with these changes. This way of looking at things challenges the assumption that religion is always stable, shared, and fully understood by those claiming to represent it.[84] And it frees us to understand the ways in which religion complicates and even frustrates meaning. The point, of course, is not to deny that religion supplies people with meaning; it no doubt does. But religion also provokes people to think differently about life and experience, and motivates as much disagreement as agreement, no matter how orthodox the creed. This fact, often overlooked, is crucial to understanding religion's tremendous fecundity throughout history.[85] And it leads me to recommend that, in future, we consider more closely how the war led people to modify or sharpen their views on religion beyond the more formulaic processes of conversion or apostasy. This may never satisfactorily explain why religion failed to stem the bloodshed, but it might do more to help us understand how war provided a salutary context for changes in religion.

83 John Horne, "Introduction: Mobilizing for 'Total War'," in *State, Society, and Mobilization in Europe during the First World War*, ed., John Horne (Cambridge: Cambridge University Press, 2002).

84 For an older, but no less incisive critique of cultural history, see Dominick LaCapra, "Is Everyone a Mentalité Case? Transference and the 'Culture' Concept," in *History and Criticism* (Ithaca: Cornell University Press, 1985).

85 James P. Carse, *The Religious Case Against Belief*.

CHAPTER FOUR
WRITING THE HISTORY OF THE "SACRED STRUGGLE" BETWEEN SCIENCE AND RELIGION

In 1896, Andrew Dickson White published *A History of the Warfare of Science with Theology in Christendom*, a two-volume landmark in the history of science. Written over the better part of two decades, the book grew out of a lecture titled "Battlefields of Science" that White gave at a variety of venues across the United States beginning in the late 1860s. Originally motivated to redress criticisms leveled against him for insisting that the newly founded Cornell University be a non-sectarian institution, White published an expanded version of the lecture as *The Warfare of Science* in 1876. He then continued working on the project for the next fifteen years, publishing sections of it regularly in *The Popular Science Monthly*. These, in turn, formed the chapters of what then became the definitive *A History of the Warfare of Science with Theology in Christendom*. Imposing in its command of the relevant literature, which was duly cited in an elaborate system of footnotes, the work was nevertheless hardly a dispassionate search for truth. On the contrary, from the first page to the last, it deployed metaphors of battle, warfare, attack, and retreat that left no doubt about White's passionate desire to see science smite its theological foes. Though White insisted that his enemy was theology and not religion, references to "the controlling minds in the Catholic Church," and to a "Protestantism [that] was ... as oppressive," strongly suggested that this was a much broader assault on existing Churches and institutional religion.[1] This fact was not lost on contemporaries, who challenged White's claim that the truth of Christianity

1   Andrew Dickson White, *A History of the Warfare of Science with Theology in Christendom*, vol. 1 (New York, 1896), 27, 60.

could be put on a surer footing by modern evolution; for in the closing pages of his work, White concluded that "out of the old welter of hopelessly conflicting statements in religion and morals has come ... the idea of a sacred literature which mirrors the most striking evolution of morals and religion in the history of our race."[2] For many, including the historian Edward Payson Evans, White had gone too far, throwing out the proverbial baby with the bathwater. If White was "not standing up for dogmatic Christianity but ... standing up for the living kernel of religion," then what, Evans asked, "constitutes this kernel?" Motivated by similar concerns, Mary Eaton wrote and asked White: "What if you succeed in creating doubts in the minds of men, in taking from them all trust in Revelation they have accepted as coming from God? What then?... What will you give us instead? A religion evolved from human brains, stripped of all that is Divine. An image without a soul?"[3] Clearly, if White aimed to save religion from theology, he left many wondering just what kind of religion this would be.

In this essay, I advocate that we take seriously White's own claim to being an unorthodox—but no less religious—innovator. In so doing, I hope to advance a different perspective not only on White, but on others who, like him, sought to advance a new religious sensibility on distinctly scientific grounds. White's history of science proclaimed the advent of a new phase in religious history. To see this however, it is necessary to focus on how White used his tools and talents as a historian to show how science benefits "true" religion. White was not a scientist, but a historian, and what has been too little understood is how he composed a history that rivaled the religious narratives he sought to displace. His vision of the course of world history was not something he could expound according to the scientific method, or corroborate using *Quellenkritik*, but expressed a faith in the unity of events and their rational explication. History, in short, had an immanent meaning, one that did not simply appear in the facts, and this essay explores how White used history as a quasi-prophetic instrument of revelation to announce a religion that had yet to happen.

Now it has long been acknowledged that White believed science could

2   Ibid., 392.
3   Glenn C. Altschuler, "From Religion to Ethics: Andrew D. White and the Dilemma of a Christian Rationalist," in *Church History* 47 (1978).

benefit religion, but only in passing, as though this really only expressed a quaint affection for a rapidly waning Christianity rather than a true conviction about the course of history and the desirability of a new religious era. Thus, Glenn Altschuler, while he acknowledges that "White did not wish to defeat religion in the name of science" and "hoped to affirm a rational, non-mythical religion," still concludes that White's demolition of the traditional foundations of Christian belief left him with little else but to affirm a sharply deracinated "humanitarian ethics."[4] For Altschuler, White's work in the history of science set him on an intellectual path "from religion to ethics" that saw in Christianity the "absolute standard of ethical conduct" and nothing more. What White himself called "pure religion and undefiled" is thus really better understood as an ethical analogue of religion, and not religion proper. In viewing White this way, of course, Altschuler affirms the reduction of religion to culture that we explored in the previous chapter. But he also engages in a broader trend in the academy dedicated to parsing religion into its supposedly core ethical constituents. This effort was especially prominent in the early twentieth century among educational reformers who hoped it might keep religious antagonisms at bay in forging a common university curriculum.[5] And it remains active today in those efforts to promote a vision of religious pluralism by claiming that all religions can be resolved into a fundamentally congruent set of ethical principles. But while there is no denying that White cites the ethical core of Christianity as the kernel that needs saving from the shell of ritual and doctrine, it is important to stress that this kernel was, for White, not just some deracinated ethical system. It was a fundamental insight into God's continuing role in history, and not merely a set of principles that could have been deduced in a purely philosophical way. To pass over White's unrepentant theism, and his claim to adding a new chapter to the sacred history of Christianity, fails to take seriously the way religions conduce to innovating in new and unpredictable ways.[6] And it illustrates just how ill-equipped we are to understand White's religious sensibility.

How does one account for White's claim to being on the threshold of a

4   Ibid., 324.
5   Stephen R. Prothero, *Religious Literacy*.
6   James P. Carse, *The Religious Case Against Belief*.

new religious era? White's conviction that science helped religion to purify itself depended on a prior conviction about history as more than merely a tool for rendering a true account of the facts; for it was only by taking stock of the unity undergirding the history of science, and the history of civilization more generally, that White was able to present science as an instrument for religion's evolution. As an interpretive matrix whose categories were immanent to the story he was telling, history was the medium of a continuing revelation. This imbrication of the sacred and secular, which sits very comfortably next to White's commitment to the protocols of objective historical research, is essential to understanding his religious sensibility. But to see it requires taking a different approach to the relationship between religion and modern historical consciousness. More specifically, it requires understanding how the fate of religion in the modern world is not just one story we tell about the course of history, but a story that history was in some ways designed to tell. Modern historical consciousness is predicated, as Reinhart Koselleck showed in his analysis of the semantics of historical time, on the transformation of "history" into the singular between roughly 1750-1850; for it is in the singular that events in history become relativized as markers of one time. In contrast with earlier modes of historical consciousness, in which events have transcendent significance and the potential to rupture time, history in the singular defines a homogenous space in which all variants of human action can be compared and judged for their relative efficacy in moving humanity forward.[7] In this space, "progress" is embodied in those forces moving history forward, and "tradition" in those holding progress back. Modern historical research and writing ever since has served an especially important role in defining this movement, and has done so by reducing religion to mundane and strictly secular motives or social functions. Thus, while history is full of stories about religion in its many varieties, modern historical consciousness is itself based on the conviction that it alone understands the dynamic of human action in a radically contingent world. This, in many ways, is the hallmark of the Enlightenment, as J. G. A. Pocock observes: "The intention of reducing or eliminating the independence of the sacred from the civil is common to so many of the phenomena we term

---

7   Reinhart Koselleck, *Futures Past: On the Semantics of Historical Time* (Cambridge, Mass.: MIT Press, 1985).

Enlightened that we may be tempted to group them all under it as the 'Enlightenment.'"[8] At the same time, this effort to supplant the active role of divine forces from history never fully succeeds in liberating history from the sacred. According to Pocock: "It can be said that historiography, the construction of an ever more complex narrative of secular circumstances, contingencies, and changes has been a principal instrument in the reduction of the divine to the human, but if 'Western' history has been related as, and through, the supersession of the sacred, it cannot be related without the constant presence of the sacred it claims to supersede."

White's *History* embodies precisely this tension between the secular and sacred. Dedicated to professional norms of objectivity and analysis, White was passionately convinced that the pursuit of historical truth revealed something about the nature of history. The history of the warfare between science and theology thus yielded both the conclusion that science must be absolutely free to pursue research, and the conviction that scientific progress was integral to the sacred struggle for religious progress; and as I read it, neither was more important than the other. White was determined to offer a true account of the warfare between science and theology precisely because he believed science offered the crucial instrument for a "gradual and healthful dissolving of this mass of unreason, [so] that the stream of 'religion pure and undefiled' may flow on broad and clear, a blessing to humanity."[9] To see these goals as complementary, rather than competing, challenges us to see that there is a faith in history that is consubstantial with the historian's craft such that history might itself be viewed as a rival religion. Constantin Fasolt makes just this point when he observes how "[e]very act of reading and writing history is ... accompanied by tacit affirmation of this creed: 'I believe that human beings are free individuals with the ability to shape their own fate and with responsibility for the consequences.' The ritual affirmation of this belief is constitutive of religion in the modern age."[10] Drawing on the work of Wittgenstein, Fasolt urges us to see how religion functions "to con-

8   J. G. A. Pocock, "Historiography and Enlightenment: A View of Their History."

9   White, *A History of the Warfare of Science with Theology in Christendom*, 322.

10   Constantin Fasolt, "History and Religion in the Modern Age," in *History and Theory* 45 (2006): 10–26.

tain the problems arising from the asymmetry between first-person and third-person statements," problems stemming from the disjunction between what people believe about the world and what they experience in it. And he reminds us that religion neutralizes this difference "by revealing the sacred will of God … [h]istory puts them at ease by revealing the sacred will of human beings." This essay explores how White sought, in his own way, to align the two by divining the religious mission of science.

Victims of Religious Persecution

Reading White today, one encounters familiar—indeed iconic—episodes intended to illustrate the relentless persecution of the scientific spirit, including the death of Bruno, the trial of Galileo, and the controversy surrounding Darwinian evolution. Likewise, one meets those heroic defenders of science like Copernicus, Kepler, and Descartes who, for White, comprised some of the "greatest men our race has produced."[11] In his account of these men and their fate, White offers what have now become stock images of the religious persecution of these scientific trail-blazers. Here the case of Galileo is paradigmatic, and White devotes considerable attention to it since, as he says, "[o]n this new champion, Galileo, the whole war [between science and theology] was at last concentrated."[12] According to White, the trouble began in 1610, when Galileo "announced that his telescope had revealed the moons of the planet Jupiter. The enemy saw that this took the Copernican theory out of the realm of hypothesis, and they gave battle immediately." To defeat him, his enemy marshaled, at different times, a "prodigious theological engine of war," including both "smaller artillery in the shape of … scriptural extracts," and the "heavy artillery … of general denunciation."[13] In their rage they even hurled "the epithets 'infidel' and 'atheist'," weapons that, for White, "can hardly be classed with civilized weapons." With great pathos, he laments:

11 White, *A History of the Warfare of Science with Theology in Christendom*, 15.
12 Ibid.,132.
13 White's battlefield imagery was reinforced by his appraisal of world affairs. See especially his *Seven Great Statesmen in the Warfare of Humanity with Unreason*.

These are burning arrows; they set fire to masses of popular prejudice, always obscuring the real question, sometimes destroying the attacking party. They are poisoned weapons. They pierce the hearts of loving women; they alienate dear children; they injure a man after life is ended, for they leave poisoned wounds in the hearts of those who loved him best—fears for his eternal salvation, dread of the Divine wrath upon him.[14]

In the face of these and other attacks, Galileo sought "[i]n vain ... to try and prove the existence of satellites by showing them to the doubters through his telescope," most of whom refused even to look. Though "the little telescope of Galileo still swept the heavens," he failed to convince his enemies "that biblical interpretation should not be applied to science." Besieged on all sides, Galileo was eventually silenced by Rome, and in a final act of humiliation was "forced to perjure himself ... and to swear that he would denounce to the Inquisition" anyone else teaching the Copernican system.

That White's account of the Galileo affair fails to do justice to the facts is well known. In his analysis of the Galileo affair, Maurice B. Finocchiaro examines how White deploys certain erroneous assumptions, the most important of which is that there was a clear divide to be made between scientific supporters and religious detractors. To be sure, Galileo and his research represented a new and provocative foray into experimental research that would force many people to think differently about how they looked at the physical world. But in his own day, one looks in vain to find either a scientific consensus defending him or a religious consensus arrayed against him. As Finocchiaro points out, there was a wide spectrum of opinion on the merits of his science as well as on the theological implications of his research, and Galileo had supporters and detractors on both sides. Indeed, in sharp contrast with the clear-cut battle lines White sketches, one must remember that Galileo received significant support from a variety of figures within the Church, including Pope Urban VIII, who was initially a patron of his work.[15] Like Finocchiaro, David Lindberg and Ronald Numbers

14 White, *A History of the Warfare of Science with Theology in Christendom*, 135.
15 Maurice A. Finocchiaro, "Science, Religion, and the Historiography of the Galileo Affair. On the Undesirability of Oversimplification," in *Osiris* 16 (2001).

argue that the crux of the debate was thus not between science and religion as we understand them. Instead, it was just as much over hermeneutics. In a post-Tridentine context, Galileo's own attempt to buttress his findings with certain passages in the Bible challenged directly the basis on which a Counter-Reformation Church sought to ground itself. Under the circumstances, such interpretive flexibility was no longer an option, since it challenged the Church's claim to be the sole correct interpreter of scripture. They thus conclude that, though "this dramatic tale has come ... to symbolize the theological assault on science," what should not be overlooked is how "[a]ll of the participants called themselves Christians, and all acknowledged biblical authority."[16]

This latter fact is crucial to correctly understanding a whole host of historical figures that White otherwise subsumes under his rubric of a mutually exclusive conflict, including Christopher Columbus and Isaac Newton. Though Columbus might not loom large as a combatant in the history of the war between science and religion, nevertheless for White, it is precisely his kind of bold spirit of discovery that embodied the overcoming of theological limitations. Therefore, he writes:

> The warfare of Columbus the world knows well: how the Bishop of Ceuta worsted him in Portugal; how sundry wise men of Spain confronted him with the usual quotations from the Psalms, from St. Paul, and from St. Augustine; how even after he was triumphant, and after his voyage had greatly strengthened the theory of the earth's sphericity ... the Church by its highest authority solemnly stumbled and persisted in going astray.[17]

What complicates this heroic picture of Columbus—namely that he persevered through such attacks because of his commitment to empirical truth—is the fact that, as David Noble points out, Columbus saw his voyages in deeply

---

16 David C. Lindberg and Ronald L. Numbers, "Beyond War and Peace: A Reappraisal of the Encounter Between Christianity and Science," in *Church History: Studies in Christianity and Culture* 55:3 (1986): 338–54.

17 White, *A History of the Warfare of Science with Theology in Christendom*, 108.

apocalyptic terms. Deriving "both his scientific geography and his apocalyptic outlook" from Pierre D'Ailly's *Imago Mundi*, Columbus was much more deeply influenced by medieval cosmology than one gleans from White's portrayal of him as a crusader for truth.[18] As Noble shows, Columbus's apocalypticism provided the basic framework for how he understood the significance of his explorations; believing that history was nearing the end of days, Columbus firmly believed that the "new" world he saw might well be the new Eden.[19] And yet, in White's treatment, Columbus is the iconoclast who is contrasted precisely with Pierre d'Ailly, whom White characterizes as "one of the most striking examples ... of a great man in theological fetters."[20]

This same effort at divesting historical figures of their religion—only to consecrate them as embodiments of a deeper "scientific" spirit of discovery—also influences how White treats Isaac Newton. In our own day, of course, it is well known that Newton was deeply enmeshed in a variety of esoteric interests.[21] For White, however, these dalliances are explained away by affirming Newton's unflagging commitment to reason. In the following passage, one can sense how hard it was for White even to conceive that Newton might be perfectly content with the variety of his interests:

> It is hard to believe that from the mind which produced the *Principia*, and which broke through the many time-honoured beliefs regarding the dates and formation of scriptural books, could have come his discussion regarding the prophecies; still,

18 White does note that Columbus possessed a copy of the *Imago Mundi*, and that he based his voyage in part on what he found there, but in a way that denies entirely Columbus's religious motivations: "It is a curious fact that this single theological error thus promoted a series of voyages which completely destroyed not only this but every other conception of geography based upon the sacred writings." See White, *A History of the Warfare of Science with Theology in Christendom*, op. cit., 112.

19 David F. Noble, *The Religion of Technology: The Divinity of Man and the Spirit of Invention*, first edition (New York: A. A. Knopf, 1997).

20 White, *A History of the Warfare of Science with Theology in Christendom*, op. cit., 107.

21 Ayval Ramati, "The Hidden Truth of Creation: Newton's Method of Fluxions," in *The British Journal for the History of Science* 34:4 (December 1, 2001): 417–38.

at various points even in this work, his power appears. From internal evidence he not only discarded the text of the Three Witnesses, but he decided that the Pentateuch must have been made up from several books....[22]

No matter what Newton's purpose, or other interests, White helps guarantee that the scientific spirit wins in the end.

Not surprisingly, a focal point of White's book is his treatment of Darwin. There, he not only misrepresents the deeply divided spectrum of opinion surrounding Darwin's work by offering glib generalizations, but actually misrepresents facts about the legendary debate between Thomas Huxley and Bishop Samuel Wilberforce in June of 1860. Their encounter, according to White, featured the following, allegedly off the cuff remarks:

> Referring to the ideas of Darwin, who was absent on account of illness ... [Bishop Wilberforce] congratulated himself in a public speech that he was not descended from a monkey. The reply came from Huxley, who said in substance: "If I had to choose, I would prefer to be a descendant of a humble monkey rather than of a man who employs his knowledge and eloquence in misrepresenting those who are wearing out their lives in the search for truth."[23]

White called Huxley's retort a "shot that reverberated through England, and indeed other countries," and his description of the episode became nothing short of a legend among scientists. But as J. R. Lucas has shown, there is sufficient discrepancy in the contemporary sources to question whether the conversation is correctly reported at all, and there is even greater evidence to suggest that Wilberforce was far more interested in taking Darwin to task for his science, than his theology. So, for example, he questioned whether there was sufficient evidence of a change in species ever having occurred, and wondered whether the sterility of hybrids wasn't evidence in favor of

22 White, *A History of the Warfare of Science with Theology in Christendom*, op. cit., 310.
23 Ibid., 70–1.

the immutability of species. Whatever the ultimate merit of these and other doubts Wilberforce had, they were legitimate questions about the empirical evidence supporting Darwin's ideas, but are ignored by White. This is because, as Lucas argues, the real issue was not about what happened—as it rarely is with legends—but with exploiting a certain version of events to maximum benefit in the context of the changing relevance of science as an institution in society. As professional scientists struggled to claim autonomy from those they increasingly saw as amateurs and dilettantes, Huxley's rejoinder to Wilberforce had all of the force of a manifesto. In contrast with the reigning assumption heretofore, namely that investigation into the nature of things was part of a larger and mutually compatible set of learned endeavors, Huxley's summary denunciation of any further cooperation signaled that scientists would henceforth increasingly police the boundaries of theirs as a professional enterprise. In this context, Huxley's remarks were as important for their style as for their content, because they gave scientists a "form of expression in their communications with the learned world" whose hallmark was professional seriousness, above all else.[24]

In spite of these manifest errors and exaggerations, we need to resist the urge simply to expose White's history as bad history. There is no question that his book makes mistakes. Some of these are garden variety mistakes that are perhaps inevitable in such a big project; others are much more serious.[25] For David Lindberg and Ronald Numbers, such mistakes show how "White read the past through battle-scarred glasses," preferring to see conflict when evidence suggested more complex interaction. Citing his treatment of Darwin, for example, they conclude that "White's seeming compulsion to reduce every episode … to a simple warlike confrontation blinded him to the possibility that Darwin's critics might have been motivated by honest scientific objections, or that his supporters might have been attracted for theological reasons."[26] Though it is essential to identify White's mistakes, I would suggest that it is not enough merely to show how White

---

24 J. R. Lucas, "Wilberforce and Huxley: A Legendary Encounter," in *The Historical Journal* 22 (1979): 313–30.

25 A good example of a serious mistake is White's misrepresentation of John Wesley as an opponent of heliocentrism.

26 Lindberg and Numbers, "Beyond War and Peace."

"and his imitators ... distorted history to serve ideological ends." We need to understand just what those ends were, and how they were served by a particular way of writing and thinking about history. In so doing, we will be in a better position to understand how this view continues to exert such a powerful hold on the public imagination.[27] While I therefore agree with Lindberg and Numbers that "discrediting the warfare thesis" is not enough, I do not follow them in seeking to "construct a satisfactory alternative" from "a more neutral starting point." In this instance, the quest for neutrality (i.e., historical "objectivity") seems particularly ill-suited to sounding the depths of White's historical desire to herald a new age of history.

The Laws and Lessons of History

White was not a professional scientist, and his conviction that science and theology necessarily conflicted was not one that he learned in the laboratory.[28] White was a historian, and his vision of the war between science and religion emerged as a function of his effort to understand convergent events in historical time and to interpret them as part of the broader course of history. Thus already in 1876, he opened *The Warfare of Science* with the following declaration:

> My thesis ... is the following: In all modern history, interference with science in the supposed interest of religion, no matter how conscientious ... has resulted in the direst evils both to religion and to science—and invariably. And on the other hand, all untrammeled scientific investigation, no matter how dangerous to religion some of its stages may have seemed, for the time, to be, has invariably resulted in the highest good of religion and of

27 For a good overview of the vexed problem of "objectivity" in history, see Peter Novick, *That Noble Dream: The Objectivity Question and the American Historical Profession* (New York: Cambridge University Press, 1988). It is significant, of course, that Novick's own approach remains very much within the boundaries of a traditional "objectivist" framework and reflects little if any concern for the theoretical issues his survey describes.

28 Frank M. Turner, "The Victorian Conflict Between Science and Religion: A Professional Dimension," in *ISIS* 69:3 (1978): 356–76.

science. I say "invariably." I mean exactly that. It is a rule to which history shows not one exception.[29]

By treating religion and science as two distinct and irreconcilable paths to truth, White offered a thesis about world history, one that he was prepared to call a law of history. And yet, White's evidence, though voluminous, was hardly comprehensive, and what he did offer came almost exclusively in the form of a focus on the brave and inspired genius who "discovers" truths about the inner workings of the physical world. Part of a strong tradition of history writing in the nineteenth century, a focus on great men and their deeds is not just a question simply of style or historical bias, but says something about how White understood the nature of history. Of course, it is a truism now to acknowledge that historians do not just report facts about the past. They select, interpret, and emplot them in ways that allow those facts to take shape as a narrative that readers can understand, as Hayden White has shown. Though White's *Metahistory* has declined in popularity in recent years, his fundamental insight still seems to me to hold true, namely: "[b]efore the historian can bring to bear upon the data of the historical field the conceptual apparatus he will use to represent and explain it, he must first prefigure the field—that is to say, constitute it as an object of mental perception."[30] And this prefigurative effort of historical consciousness is "indistinguishable from the linguistic act in which the field is made ready for interpretation as a domain of a particular kind." The decisive "prefigurative effort" in this instance, of course, is to characterize the choice confronting individuals between science and theology as a mutually dichotomous and exhaustive one. By telling the history of science in this way White reduced scientific discovery to what Simon Schaffer calls "single events of individual mental labor whose analysis requires the examination of logical or psychological maneuvers." Shorn of their connection to broader contexts, convictions, or inner conflicts, such maneuvers are presented as so many ratchet-like advances along the line of progress. As just such "an heroic model of discovery in which analysis concentrates on the

29 Andrew Dickson White, *The Warfare of Science* (London: King & Co., 1876).
30 Hayden V. White, *Metahistory: The Historical Imagination in Nineteenth-Century Europe* (Baltimore: Johns Hopkins University Press, 1973).

inspired genius," White's narrative gives both "an account of how science changes" and how history works.[31]

By portraying science as the activity of the lone mind, White frames the relationship between science and religion as a strict either/or, rather than as a fluid, complementary, or potentially contradictory relationship between multiple desires. But the focus on individuals, in turn, provides what he takes to be the proof for an intractable pattern of movement in history that transcends individuals. For if every example he analyzes can be reduced to a simple story of contending deep impulses—truth vs. dogma, courage vs. fear, science vs. religion—then the story of individuals is really the story of humanity itself; individuals and their struggles serve merely as exemplars of a deeper truth in history. This Manichean vision of opposing forces is clearly evident in the following description of the rise of modern medicine, where White writes:

> Men of science also rose, in the stricter sense of the word, even in the centuries under the most complete sway of theological thought and ecclesiastical power; a science, indeed, alloyed with theology, but still infolding [sic] precious germs. Of these were men … all of whom cultivated sciences subsidiary to medicine, and in spite of charges of sorcery, with possibilities of imprisonment and death, kept the torch of knowledge burning, and passed it on to future generations. From the Church itself, even when the theological atmosphere was most dense, rose here and there men who persisted in something like scientific effort.[32]

Or consider his way of summarizing the origins of modern meteorology:

> But at a very early period we see the beginning of a scientific view. In Greece, the Ionic philosophers held that such phenomena are obedient to law. Plato, Aristotle, and many lesser lights, attempted to account for them on natural grounds; and their

31 Simon Schaffer, "Scientific Discoveries and the End of Natural Philosophy," in *Social Studies of Science* 16:3 (1986): 387–420.
32 White, *A History of the Warfare of Science with Theology in Christendom*, op. cit., 34.

explanations, though crude, were based upon observation and thought.... But, as the Christian Church rose to power, this evolution was checked; the new leaders of thought found, in the Scriptures recognized by them as sacred, the basis for a new view, or rather for a modification of the old view.[33]

In both these passages science and theology contend, not merely for rational assent on the part of individuals, but for the space of history as such. In the classic sense of a zero-sum game, White treats a gain for one as automatically a loss for the other, and so it goes throughout history. Though he acknowledges the fact that there are men within the Church who have sometimes been drawn to science, this happens in spite of their theological convictions and is never nourished by them. By approaching history in this way White weaves together a horizon against which so many "logical or psychological maneuvers" can be compared and contrasted in order to establish the inevitable progress of science.

This presumes, of course, that what is compared is, in fact, comparable; that there exists a "space" or medium that enables comparison and that enables one to discriminate between mutually exclusive and exhaustive options. According to sociologist and historian of science Bruno Latour, rendering science and religion as locked in a pitched battle that amounts to a zero-sum game is the result of an unremitting purification of human rationality from any admixture of superstition. The relentless separating and purifying of human life and values from allegedly non-human ones produces a "modern constitution" that separates "nature" from "culture" and issues in a smooth, unremitting modern temporality:

The impression of passing irreversibly is generated only when we bind together the cohort of elements that make up our day-to-day universe. It is their systematic cohesion, and the replacement of these elements by others rendered just as coherent in the subsequent period, which gives us the impression of time that passes, of a continuous flow going from the future toward the past....[34]

33 Ibid., 333.
34 Ibid., 72.

This is a process less *in* history than *of* history, however, since liberating "humanity" from nature and religion constitutes the threshold of modernity:

> Modernity is often defined in terms of humanism, either as a way of saluting the birth of "man" or as a way of announcing his death. But this habit itself is modern, because it remains asymmetrical. It overlooks the simultaneous birth of "nonhumanity"—things, object, or beasts—and the equally strange beginning of a crossed-out God, relegated to the sidelines. Modernity arises first from the conjoined creation of those three entities, and then from the masking of the conjoined birth and the separate treatment of the three communities while, underneath, hybrids continue to multiply as an effect of this separate treatment.[35]

And yet, for all this, the long list of exceptions to the rules laid down by the modern constitution throws its fundamental premises into question, and motivates Latour to suggest that, in the end, we "have never been modern" in spite of ourselves.

The proliferation of "quasi-objects," whose hallmark is that they belong to multiple temporalities and so fall outside of the flow of modern time, is no minor matter. Quasi-objects "mix up different periods, ontologies or genres," and can be integrated into modern self-understanding only as anomalies and only under certain circumstances. In our own day, according to Latour, the "proliferation of quasi-objects has exploded modern temporality":

> First there were the skyscrapers of postmodern architecture ... then Khomeini's Islamic revolution, which no one managed to peg as revolutionary or reactionary. From then on, the exceptions have popped up without cease. No one can now categorize actors that belong to the "same time" in a single coherent group. No one knows any longer whether the reintroduction of the

35 Bruno Latour, *We Have Never Been Modern* (Cambridge, Mass.: Harvard University Press, 1993).

bear in the Pyrenees, kolkhozes, aerosols, the Green Revolution, the anti-smallpox vaccine, Star Wars, the Muslim religion, partridge hunting, the French Revolution, service industries, labor unions, cold fusion, Bolshevism, relativity, Slovak nationalism, commercial sailboats, and so on, are outmoded, up to date, futuristic, atemporal, nonexistent, or permanent.[36]

Of course, by rendering science and religion as mutually exclusive and exhaustive categories, White guarantees that the struggle between them produces the appearance of the necessity of forward historical movement. In this, he plays his part in shoring up the modern constitution. At the same time, what I see as the decidedly religious impetus behind his attack against theology might be viewed as an instance of what Latour calls a "quasi-object": a phenomenon that undermines the neat divisions between modern/pre-modern.[37]

White was not primarily concerned to track the rise of institutions promoting scientific activity or the refinement of method. He was not interested in the evolution of new scientific instruments or the global diffusion of knowledge among networks of scientists. His goal was to establish "science" and "religion" as trans-historical categories, for it is precisely as trans-historical realities that science and religion come into competition and take on colossal, world-historical, proportions as part of the divine plan.[38] He attests

36 Ibid.
37 When viewed in conjunction with these other quasi-objects, White's bid for a new religious future makes sense, or at least a different kind of sense, but only if we are prepared to "pass from one temporality to another," one that "does not oblige us to use the labels 'archaic' or 'advanced.'" Can we imagine a history that explores the past, as it unfolded in all of its complexity, but from a present that no longer assumes an inexorable distance from the past? Is it possible, as Latour suggests, to "regroup the contemporary elements along a spiral rather than a line"? Might we view the past as "not surpassed but revisited, repeated, surrounded, protected, recombined, reinterpreted and reshuffled?" This imaginative effort seems to me to be absolutely necessary if we are to better assess the historical import of the kind of deep faith in science White and others had, and so many still have. Latour, *We Have Never Been Modern*, op. cit., 75.
38 Peter Harrison, *The Territories of Science and Religion* (University of Chicago Press, 2015).

to this goal in a number of shorter essays where he addresses religion and science and their potentially regenerative role to the progress of civilization. In a review of two continental works of "universal history" published in 1857, a young White insisted on the primacy of universal education to the liberal arts. "A good Universal History is not a dry commentary ... [b]ut it is what may serve as a foundation for all special study of history, or philosophy, or politics—what may counteract the mechanical tendency to study single points—what may lift the new race of young men above the plane of our old demagogues...."[39] To achieve a "healthy mental discipline" it was crucial to immerse oneself in the kind of history in which "the story of a country is made Life," for "God is ever giving growth through all new light from new history." In *The Message of the Nineteenth Century to the Twentieth*, published in 1883, White lamented the prevalence of a mercantilist spirit in American society, and declared that "the great thing to be done is neither more nor less than to develop above all things other great elements of civilization now held in check which shall take their rightful place in the United States, which shall modify the mercantile spirit."[40] Important "counter-elements of civilization" included philosophy, religion, science, literature, and art, but White insisted that their animating spirit be an "ideal of a new and better civilization." If refashioned correctly, these elements could each contribute to regenerating American civilization. Thus, with respect to religion and science more specifically, White declared: "In the individual minds and hearts and souls of the messengers who are now preparing for the next century is the source of regeneration. They must form an ideal of religion higher than a life devoted to grasping and grinding and griping with a whine for mercy at the end of it. They must form an ideal of science higher than increasing the production of iron or cotton goods."[41] That historians, such as himself, had a decisive role to play in fostering a new, revitalized civilization was the impulse behind White's 1884 essay *On Studies in General History*

39 Andrew Dickson White, "Glimpses of a Universal History," in *The New Englander* 15 (1857), 427.

40 Andrew Dickson White, *The Message of the Nineteenth Century to the Twentieth: An Address Delivered Before the Class of 1853 in the Chapel of Yale College, 26 June 1883* (Tuttle, Morehouse & Taylor, 1883).

41 Ibid., 24.

and the History of Civilization. In this paean to big "H"istory, White stressed that comprehensive studies must move beyond mere summary. "The great deep ground out of which large historical studies grow is the ethical ground—the simple ethical necessity for the perfecting, first, of man as man, and, secondly, of man as a member of society; or, in other words, the necessity for the development of humanity on the one hand and society on the other."[42] By divining the "laws of religious, moral, intellectual, social, and political health or disease," the study of the history of civilization can help individuals and groups play a role in the evolution of a better future.

White's stress on the "ethical ground" of historical study, when viewed alongside his conviction that religion should progress beyond "a life devoted to grasping and grinding," can and has been interpreted as endorsing a purification of "religion" into "ethics." On this view, White's thought represents more of a progressive de-Christianized ethics of universal brotherhood than "real religion." The historical trappings of revealed religion are exposed as mythical ways of defining the best ethical impulses to live together peaceably. This is Altschuler's view, who characterizes White as moving "from religion to ethics," and who draws support for this interpretation from White's biography. Thus Altschuler points to the decisive fact that White was raised in a nonconformist Christian household, whose "gentle humanism" and "absolute standard of ethical conduct" had a lasting influence on his whole life.[43] I want to argue otherwise. To be sure, one way of understanding "the simple ethical necessity for the perfecting" of civilization and its components—at least *vis-a-vis* religion—is to see it as a process of distillation. Religion will only serve again as a noble goal after a process of winnowing away superstition, intolerance, the dead hand of ritual, and the like. And this view is seemingly reinforced by White in particularly forceful terms in the essay *Evolution and Revolution*, published in 1890:

> What then shall we glorify? What shall be the ideal of political
> conduct? The answer is simple: let us glorify the evolution of a

42 Andrew Dickson White, *On Studies in General History and the History of Civilization* (Putnam, 1885).

43 Altschuler, "From Religion to Ethics: Andrew D. White and the Dilemma of a Christian Rationalist."

strong moral sense in individuals and nations of well-being and well-doing; of clear and honest thinking; of right reason; of high purpose; of bold living up to one's thought, reason, and purpose; let us glorify these, let these be our ideals. And what shall be the aim of practical effort? The answer to this question, too, is simple: let us strive to clear the way for a steady, healthful evolution; for the unfolding of a better future.[44]

Reason and morality are what remain when religion is taken away, when it is, as Charles Taylor has put it, "subtracted" in such a way as to reveal the putatively more basic, underlying fundaments of human life and society. And yet, like all subtraction stories, this conclusion requires that one ignore the formative role of religion in shaping precisely these forms of reason and morality in the first place.[45] This way of reading White also depends very much on how one interprets what White means by "evolution." If, by evolution, one takes White to mean a growing and deepening appreciation of what mature humans are capable of doing on their own, then "the evolution of a strong moral sense" is probably best seen as the result of a paring away of religion. If evolution means something different however, namely, a process of development immanent to history itself, then White might be seen as pointing to a transformation of religion in history. And this transformation, though profoundly altering traditional manifestations of religion, might just as well be interpreted as "religious," in contrast to a definitive move from "religion" in the direction of ethics. Let us examine this matter more closely.

The standardization, in our own day, of evolution as a term firmly connected with the research of Darwin, is misleading when trying to understand what evolution might have meant for White. In the essay *Evolution and Revolution*, White defines his terms in the following way:

> [W]e distinguish between two uses of the word Evolution: first, its larger use, which includes every sort of development, regular

44 Andrew Dickson White, *Evolution and Revolution: An Address Delivered at the Annual Commencement of the University of Michigan: June 26, 1890* (The University, 1890).
45 Charles Taylor, *A Secular Age*, 26–29.

or irregular, rapid or slow, revolutionary or of natural growth; secondly, its more restricted use, which confines it to the more regular, natural processes, to growth in the main, quiet, steady, and peaceful. In this latter restricted sense I shall use the word evolution in this address, and I purpose to deal with the distinction between development by natural growth and development by catastrophe—between progress by evolution and progress by revolution."[46]

What needs to be observed here, of course, is that evolution was just as liable to be understood as violent revolution as slow growth, hence the need to clarify terms. Among those events that counted as revolutionary, of course, White cited the American and French revolutions, and the Civil War. He also cited contemporary revolutionary pressures building in Russia. In all these cases progress comes at such a high price that one is forced to ask: is this a "necessary law of human progress? Must the future of mankind be no better than the past in this respect?"[47] In answer to this question White cites multiple instances of slow, evolutionary progress, what he called "steady, healthful evolution" and the "unfolding of a better future." Slow but steady progress in material conditions, art, literature, government, law, and morality all attest to deeper evolutionary possibilities of progress without "catastrophe." This, it seems to me, is the way to read White's approach to the evolution of religion in history. Instead of necessarily succumbing to a winnowing or disenchantment, religion contains the potential for progenitive transformation—evolution from within. Instead of being subtracted from history, religion evolves as the result of powerful, if hidden, forces, a process immanent to religion's unfolding in history. Without saying so explicitly, White suggests as much in a section on "evolution in religion" that closes the essay. There, he posits, once again, a "contrast between advance by revolution and advance by evolution." For White, the "modern attempt at advance by revolution is seen in a thousand horrors; in the terrible Thirty Years' War; in the religious wars of France; in the driving out of the Protestants from Austria, of the Huguenots from France," and multiple other

46 Ibid., 13.
47 Ibid., 11.

painful and bloody episodes. At the same time, however, he calls attention to religion's

> advance in modern history by more steady evolution, through the efforts of Melanchthon, Contarini, and Cranmer, of the Wesleys, Edwards, Bishop Butler, and Channing, of Emerson, Theodore Parker and Newman, of Arnold, Maurice, and Robertson—working indeed apparently at cross purposes, but each leaving something for the enrichment of the world, and all together, no matter what their purpose, enforcing more and more upon the world the idea that dogmas and metaphysics are but the mere husks and rinds enclosing the precious kernel of truth.[48]

Though White opposes here the "husks" of dogma to the "kernel of truth," the list of religious innovators he cites hardly suggests a group whose goal is to define a deracinated, universal ethics somehow different in substance from religion. It is also a group that so clearly gives the lie to his claim that it is theology that is the enemy, and not religion. Though White refers disparagingly to "dogmas and metaphysics," he does not endorse anything approaching an unmitigated secularism. On the contrary, he cautions a middle way between conservatives and radicals. He is particularly afraid of "extreme radicals" who "too frequently produce, prematurely, a vacuum sure to be filled by some new belief more absurd than the old." Against the threat of these "ultraists," White points to "those who are laboring for a more quiet, beautiful, and effective evolution of religious thought and effort." Imitating the life of "the Master," these defenders of Christianity lead "simple and beautiful lives, preaching ... great vitalizing truths, devoting themselves more and more to the essentials of religion." That this group runs the entire range of Christian thought and practice confirms that these "vitalizing truths," though cutting across denominational lines, are fundamentally Christian. They are, moreover, thoroughly historical, and do not hover outside time. Indeed, given his desire to define evolutionary processes that are "in the main, quiet, steady, and peaceful," it is clear that White is

48   Ibid., 32.

talking about an immanent evolutionary process in the history of religion. White thus concludes:

> The steady evolution of humanity in all these vast and various fields demands at times struggles, and even hard fighting; but it also demands, and far more constantly, the development of the great silent forces which are frequently the most powerful forces. Volcanoes explode, earthquakes come and go, but the steady power of gravitation never ceases. While battles must be fought, at times with great din and suffering, truths must be discovered, developed and spread.[49]

Viewed in this way, White's pursuit of the "kernel of truth" in religion involves far more than merely stripping extraneous trappings away to reveal a purely ethical core.

A "Sacred Struggle"

Though White did much to create the impression of an inherent conflict between science and religion, it must be remembered that he belonged to an era that still believed very much in the goodness of a "creator God" who would not deceive people about his true nature, or the world he created for them.[50] As he writes in *The Warfare of Science*: "God's truths must agree, whether discovered by looking within upon the soul, or without upon the world. A truth written upon the human heart to-day, in its full play of emotions or passions, cannot be at any real variance even with a truth written upon a fossil whose poor life ebbed forth millions of years ago."[51] The appearance of conflict therefore is really only the result of a flawed way of apprehending the otherwise orderly universe. When understood correctly, science revealed the essentially evolutionary character of all life and creation, and when

---

49 Ibid., 34–35.
50 R. Laurence Moore, *Touchdown Jesus: The Mixing of Sacred and Secular in American History*, op. cit., 133.
51 White, *The Warfare of Science*.

complemented by the best recent biblical scholarship, actually laid the foundation for "the idea of a sacred literature which mirrors the most striking evolution of morals and religion in the history of our race."[52] The progressive thrust of science liberated "pure religion" to take its rightful place in the future:

> However overwhelming then, the facts may be which Anthropology, History, and their kindred sciences may, in the interest of simple truth, establish against the theological doctrine of "the Fall"; however completely they may fossilize various dogmas, catechisms, creeds, confessions, "plans of salvation" and "schemes of redemption," which have been evolved from the great minds of the theological period: science, so far from making inroads on religion, or even upon our Christian development of it, will strengthen all that is essential in it, giving new and nobler paths to man's highest aspirations. For the one great, legitimate scientific conclusion of anthropology is, that, more and more, a better civilization of the world, despite all its survivals of savagery and barbarism, is developing men and women on whom the declarations of the nobler Psalms, of Isaiah, of Micah, the Sermon on the Mount, the first great commandment, and the second, which is like unto it, St. Paul's praise of charity and St. James's definition of "pure religion and undefiled," can take stronger hold for the more effective and more rapid uplifting of our race.[53]

Far from sounding the death knell of religion, science revealed a surer foundation for a new religious era. In this context, one needs to see White as deeply committed to what he himself called the "sacred struggle for the liberty of science." Science illuminated the deeper truths of religion as much as it revealed the laws governing the physical world. It perfected religious insight, and helped lay the foundation for a true grasp of revelation. Thus he claimed:

52 Ibid., 394.
53 Ibid., 322.

If, then, modern science in general has acted powerfully to dissolve away the theories and dogmas of the older theologic interpretation, it has also been active in a reconstruction and recrystallization of truth; and very powerful in this reconstruction have been the evolution doctrines which have grown out of the thought and work of men like Darwin and Spencer. In the light thus obtained the sacred text has been transformed: out of the old chaos has come order; out of the old welter of hopelessly conflicting statements in religion and morals has come, in obedience to this new conception of development, the idea of a sacred literature which mirrors the most striking evolution of morals and religion in the history of our race.[54]

If White concluded that sacred scripture was now better viewed as sacred "literature," he nevertheless also saw this change in perspective was divinely ordained. For he insisted that it was "only possible under that divine light which the various orbs of science have done so much to bring into the mind and heart and soul of man—a revelation, not of the Fall of Man, but of the Ascent of Man—an exposition, not of temporary dogmas and observances, but of the Eternal Law of Righteousness—the one upward path of individuals and for nations."[55] Does this sound like someone committed to destroying religion? Hardly. This passage and others like it clearly show that White is not heralding a purely scientific age, but a new religious one.

To write the history of a new religious age as the product of "a quiet and steady evolution," required a delicate handling of events that were, strictly speaking, not solely contingent on human acts and motives. This explains White's preference for using metaphors drawn from nature to convey the workings of Providence. Indeed, to depict the "development of the great silent forces" driving history, one had to understand "the steady power of gravitation [that] never ceases."[56] Thus the rise of science, which at first appears as the result of individual geniuses and their tireless devotion to truth, is revealed at a deeper level to resemble more a force of nature. This

54 Ibid., 394.
55 Ibid., 395.
56 White, *Evolution and Revolution,* op. cit., 64.

is everywhere evident where White refers to "the germs of a fruitful skepticism" that give birth to the scientific spirit, and how it became nearly impossible to "arrest the swelling tide" of scientific progress.[57] In a related metaphor, White writes how the "current of evolutionary thought could not ... be checked: dammed up for a time, it broke out in new channels and in ways and places least expected." By assigning agency to science *cum* nature, rather than individuals, White linked scientific progress to the unfolding of Providence. This does not contradict his stress on individual scientific geniuses. On the contrary, it helps to establish the transcendent significance of the "event" of scientific enlightenment. Consider how White describes Darwin's discovery:

> The scientific world realizes, too, more and more, the power of character shown by Darwin in all this great career; the faculty of silence, the reserve of strength seen in keeping his great thought—his idea of evolution by natural selection—under silent study and meditation for nearly twenty years, giving no hint of it to the world at large, but working in every field to secure proofs or disproofs, and accumulating masses of precious material for the solution of the questions involved.[58]

This portrait of a man absolutely devoted to quiet research was crucial for effectively immunizing him from any motives other than pure science. It is, in turn, crucial for setting the stage effectively for Darwin's "breakthrough," an event that White describes—in nothing short of a rhetorical crescendo—as providential: "Not until fourteen years later occurred the event which showed him that the fullness of time had come—the letter from Alfred Russel Wallace, to whom, in brilliant researches during the decade from 1848 to 1858 ... the same truth of evolution by natural selection had been revealed."[59] For White, it is events expressing "the fullness of time" that reveal the truth to Darwin; it is not Darwin who causes events. And only the cultivation of proper, patient, and passive receptivity allowed Darwin to receive the truth.

57 White, *A History of the Warfare of Science with Theology in Christendom.*
58 Ibid., 66–67.
59 Ibid., 67.

White's reference to religious motifs is more than metaphorical. Their invocation at key moments frames the story he telling as one of religious significance. Readers are supposed to understand what happens when science is pursued falsely in order to all the more appreciate the role God played in putting science back on course. Recalling the Old Testament flood, in both its punitive and regenerative aspects, White characterizes the shift to a Darwinian world in the following terms:

> As the great dogmatic barrier between the old and new views of the universe was broken down, the flood of new thought pouring over the world stimulated and nourished strong growths in every field of research and reasoning: edition after edition of the book was called for … the stagnation of scientific thought, which Buckle, only a few years before had lamented gave place to a widespread and fruitful activity; masses of accumulated observations, which had seemed stale and unprofitable, were made alive; facts formerly without meaning now found their interpretation.[60]

Though White never explicitly spoke of himself in this way, it is perhaps not unwarranted to interpret him as seeking to evangelize the good news of science. Looking at things this way might also go some way towards explaining his otherwise puzzling reticence to engage with critics, many of whom seemed to sense all too well the theological import of his conclusions. In his correspondence, White was keenly aware that his bid to save religion by allowing science to demolish theology was fraught with paradox. But unlike Altschuler, who calls this "White's dilemma," I would suggest that replying "weakly that he was doing his best to save the Bible" was not a contradiction, but fully consistent with "his aim … to provide a new stronger basis for the Christian religion."[61] Rather than assume that his "long and embarrassing exchange with Evans indicates all that he had to say about religion," as Altschuler does, it seems to me just as defensible to

60 Ibid., 68.
61 Altschuler, "From Religion to Ethics: Andrew D. White and the Dilemma of a Christian Rationalist," op. cit.

suggest that White considered it important not to say too much. Unlike scholars, prophets must take care to foster the impression that they are passive conduits for divine insight into the order of things. If, for some, "White fell short in his attempt to strengthen religion and kindled fear about the future course of Christianity and society," then avoiding debate might just as easily be taken as a sign of his faith that what he was writing was, in the last instance, not his story, but one with divine origins.

Conclusion

Andrew Dickson White was profoundly concerned about the future of religion, and his analysis of history was as much concerned with the fate of religion as the rise of science. One might even argue that he was an evangelist in his own right, seeking to transcend religion in the name of better religion. In this, he was not unlike Auguste Comte, who envisioned science helping to promote a new religion of humanity in the final stage of history. He might also be compared with Thomas Huxley, who, as Bernard Lightman shows, "asserted that the revolution effected in the modern mind by the beneficial impact of science represented the final climax of the Protestant Reformation."[62] Or Ernest Rénan, who did not just claim for his "religion … the progress of science," but sought to infuse the progress of science with religious drama.[63] Like these men, White believed that he "represented the bravery and independence … of the intellectual who realized in his work something more important, something quasi-divine."[64] But like them, he is almost universally treated as a foe of religion because his portrait of the intolerance, inconsistencies, and excesses of religion seems so devastating as to preclude taking seriously anything else he might say about the future of religion. This is a blind spot that is endemic, not only to history, but to sociology and so many other social science accounts that took up the question of religion in the nineteenth century. The case of Comte and sociology

62 Bernard Lightman, "Victorian Sciences and Religions: Discordant Harmonies," in *Osiris* 6 (2001): 343–66.
63 Ernest Renan, *The Future of Science* (Roberts Brothers, 1893).
64 Alan Pitt, "The Cultural Impact of Science in France: Ernest Renan and the Vie De Jesus," in *The Historical Journal* 43 (2000): 79–101.

is perhaps best illustrative of the dilemma. Having concluded that religion was a primitive phase of thought whose function was to secure social cohesion, Comte held that the evolution of thinking must needs pass through phases of increasing rational purification—but retain the same function of securing social cohesion. Thus, in spite of its commitment to objectivity and scientific rigor, sociology internalized the erstwhile functions of religion to serve as an "alternative ideology that would also function as a source of values, albeit values that were grounded 'scientifically'."[65] Though sociology and cognate social sciences, including history, have done much to achieve a level of critical self-reflexivity, reflected in careful empirical research and avowals of value-neutrality, they still "bear within them an incipient anti-religious bias" that is seemingly "built into the DNA of the discipline," as Peter Harrison observes. Value neutrality is compromised at the most basic level by their conviction to have superseded—and replaced—religion.

To be sure, White evinced no impulse towards orthodoxy or Church-building of any kind, and there are many who will be skeptical of my attempt to portray him as a religious innovator. Let me attempt to bolster my argument by suggesting how this too might be viewed as an instance of devotional activism. In previous chapters, I showed how some nineteenth-century Catholics responded to their critics by explicitly embracing tactics that mirrored those of their foes. This kind of devotional activism features a mutual entanglement in similar strategies—fought in the same time over the same stakes—that complicates any attempt to dismiss these efforts as backward or reactionary. Can we see White engaged in a similar kind of maneuver? I think we can. Of course, White was firmly convinced that the history of science illustrated how science alone was the arbiter of empirical truth, and that it could never be rivalled or supplanted by "theology" (construed as the formal rules embodied in official religious institutions). At the same time, he bolstered his claim by referring repeatedly—and earnestly—to Providence as ensuring the course of history would ultimately vindicate science AND reveal it to be part of a "sacred struggle" for truth revealing the benevolence and rationality of a creator God. But he did not believe, as ardent

65 Peter Harrison, "Religion, Innovation and Secular Modernity," in *Religion and Innovation: Antagonists or Partners?* ed., Donald Yerxa (London: Bloomsbury, 2015): 76.

materialists did, that science thereby nullified a belief in providence or a divine creator. And so, one way to view what White is doing is to see it as deploying a model of supersession—akin to the materialist account of science supplanting religion—as a way of showing how science purified and preserved "true" from "false" religion. In this, he joined others, like E. B. Taylor, J. G Frazer—and Franz Brentano, as we shall see in the next chapter—in viewing religion as "a form of primitive science, destined to be superseded by the genuine article."[66]

The goal of this essay has not been to accuse White of being insincere, or to unmask him as a closet orthodox Christian. He was neither. His faith in scientific progress was real and he was a sincere and even harsh critic of dogmatic Christianity, but not in the name of some unmitigated secularism. White was serious about preparing humanity to accept the new revelation that was science, a revelation that could only take place in the "fullness of time." To grasp this, it is essential that we take stock of how his *History* was indelibly shaped by what can only be called religious forces that he saw as complementing and not contradicting science. It is essential that we find new and creative ways of understanding this kind of religious sensibility without obligating ourselves to staying within the overly schematic terms of the conflict thesis that White himself did so much to shape. White's account of the historical rise of science was actually a much more complex plea for better religion. While I am not proposing that we treat White as a Luther or Melancthon, I do think that it makes more sense to take him seriously as a religious innovator instead of simply dismissing his religious efforts as marginal to his more important work as a historian. In this instance they were mutually overlapping, and this fact complicates our understanding of what is perhaps the real issue underlying these events, namely: the vexed role of the historian as a prophet of modernity. In the end, what should not be overlooked is how White's account of the "warfare between science and theology" maps the modern differently, that is to say, from within a distinctly religious vision of the future.[67] This may or may not help

66 Harrison, "Religion, Innovation, and Secular Modernity," op. cit., 76.
67 For a defense of the need to adopt a new view of the multiple trajectories of modernity, see S. N. Eisenstadt, ed., *Multiple Modernities* (New York: Transaction Publishers, 2002).

explain the hold his vision of conflict continues to exert on our social imaginary. But it does help us see the need for cultivating a better historical sensibility in how we approach the history of the conflict between science and religion. If we are to understand how science and religion have become locked in a struggle of epic—indeed, world-historical proportions—then a task of the first order will be to lay bare the foundations of this debate, which includes understanding the role of history and historians in its making.

CHAPTER FIVE
FRANZ BRENTANO, JEWS,
AND THE "NEW CHRISTIANITY"

Franz Brentano was a major figure in the philosophical scene of Central Europe during the late nineteenth and early twentieth centuries, who helped influence the founding of such important intellectual movements as phenomenology, analytic philosophy, and psychoanalysis. A former Catholic priest, he spent his early career at the University of Würzburg before leaving holy orders and taking up a professorship of philosophy at the University of Vienna. This essay offers a fresh interpretation of Franz Brentano's life and career in Vienna between 1874 and 1895. More specifically, it explores some of the circumstances surrounding Brentano's controversial *My Last Wishes for Austria*, which recounts his battle with the Austrian government to have him reinstated as a full professor of philosophy. The failure to regain his professorship was more than a career setback that embittered Brentano. It was the occasion for him to publicly declare the backwardness of Catholic Austria. I will try to show how this condemnation was shaped by Brentano's specific experience as an apostate priest at the intersection of Catholic and Jewish segments of Viennese society, and nourished by his views on the course of history. In this way, this essay seeks to enrich our understanding of the interplay between Brentano's life and thought, and add another chapter to our understanding of the Viennese *fin-de-siècle*.

From Würzburg to Vienna

When Brentano arrived in Vienna in 1874, he was thirty-six years old. He had just published *Psychology From an Empirical Standpoint*, his third book, and had been appointed full professor of philosophy at the University. Though he later credited Hermann Lotze with helping him secure the post,[1] it is clear from letters to his friend and former student Carl Stumpf that his mother also played an important part in devising the plan, and used family connections in Vienna to secure her son's appointment.[2] Indeed, far from a "surprise," the call to Vienna was a near constant subject of conversation between him and Stumpf, with Brentano understandably anxious about the potential fallout over his having left the priesthood.[3] This fear was nothing if not justified, as Brentano himself later recalled. In a letter to Hermann Schell from 1885, Brentano reports "not having known how, as I spoke, I stood on a virtual volcano that threatened to erupt at any moment."[4] For it turned out that Brentano's first public lecture, *On the Reasons for Discouragement in the Field of Philosophy*, was attended by no small number of listeners eager to expose his "Jesuitical character" and create a public outcry that would make it impossible for him to accept his new appointment.[5] Brentano was nevertheless able to win over the packed audience of between four and five hundred in the university *Aula*, and finished the lecture to thunderous applause.

Between 1874 and 1880, Brentano lived the life of a bachelor-scholar, first taking up residence in a small apartment in the *Fürstenhof Hotel* at Beatrixgasse 19, and then moving to a larger apartment at Erdbergstrasse 19, where he hosted students interested in continuing philosophical discussions begun in class. A charismatic teacher and person, Brentano cultivated a loyal following among students, and likewise became a welcome and frequent guest in some of the most fashionable houses in Vienna. He was especially celebrated for his penchant for inventing riddles and his chess-playing ability. Brentano was not without his critics, however. There

1   Josef Hasenfuß, *Hermann Schell als Wegbereiter zum II. Vatikanischen Konzil. Sein Briefwechsel mit Franz Brentano* (Paderborn: Schöningh, 1978), 53.
2   Franz Clemens Brentano, Peter Goller, and Gerhard Oberkofler, *Briefe an Carl Stumpf, 1867–1917* (Akademie Druck u. Verlag, 1989), 43. In particular, Emilie Brentano appealed to Heinrich von Gagern, the liberal champion of a *Grossdeutsch* solution to the national question and Hessian envoy to the Austrian empire.
3   In a letter to Schell, Brentano refers to the call to Vienna as a "surprise." See Schell, *Wegbereiter*, 44.
4   Ibid., 44.
5   Schell, *Wegbereiter*, op. cit.

was a strong antipathy towards him in certain clerical circles, including the powerful Cardinal Joseph Rauscher, and some delighted in claiming that Brentano only left the priesthood because he couldn't bear the demands of celibacy.[6] But there were other criticisms as well, from non-clerical circles. Robert A. Kann, for example, cites the playwright Alfred von Berger as saying that Brentano rejected papal infallibility because he couldn't stand the idea of anyone other than himself being infallible.[7] There were also more light-hearted jabs, such as the letter in which Heinrich Gomperz pokes fun at Brentano's penchant for near-constant philosophizing and "solving the mystery of life."[8] And there is the novella by Adolf Wilbrandt, *Der Gast vom Abendstern*, whose "other-worldly" Professor Hamann was modelled on Brentano. Depicted as a uniquely spiritual, charismatic, but also effeminate character, Hamann-as-Brentano called forth no shortage of defenders who stressed Brentano's masculinity.[9] There is, of course, also the fact that Brentano could be very critical, and alienated students who deviated too much from the path set by their teacher. In spite of the tendency today to talk of a Brentano school, Brentano himself lamented later in life that "almost all of my students have turned away from me, the one for this reason, the other for that reason, most for dishonorable, even laughable, reasons."[10] At the same time, Brentano was a devoted friend and mentor, who was

6   Brentano discusses this rumor in a letter to his cousin Georg von Hertling. The unpublished, undated letter is found in the Houghton Library Archive at Harvard University (bMs 216).

7   Theodor Gomperz, Heinrich Gomperz, and Robert Adolf Kann, *Theodor Gomperz: ein Gelehrtenleben im Bürgertum der Franz-Josefs-Zeit: Auswahl seiner Briefe und Aufzeichnungen, 1869–1912, erläutert und zu einer darstellung seines Lebens verknüpft von Heinrich Gomperz* (Wien: Österreichische Akademie der Wissenschaften, 1974), 76.

8   Ibid., 249.

9   Adolf Wilbrandt, "Der Gast Vom Abendstern," in *Novellen aus der Heimat* (Stuttgart: Cotta, 1891), 61–118.

10   Schell, *Wegbereiter*, op. cit., 76. Brentano was critical of the idea that he was the founder of a school. Carl Stumpf notes this fact, but nevertheless goes on to add: "And yet, if he encountered basic intuitions in his students' publications which were considerably different from his own, and which were not thoroughly justified and defended on the spot, he was inclined to consider them at first as unmotivated, arbitrary statements even though they may have

quick to apologize and did his best to mend fences, even after years of not corresponding.

Brentano's singular dedication to philosophy was famous, and helps to explain both the adulation he received from students as well as the tendency towards strife with those same students whom he envisioned as emissaries of his philosophy. It also explains the fact that much of his published work consisted of smaller scientific works dedicated to individual problems rather than large, overarching systematic tomes. During his Viennese period, Brentano published a variety of works, including the book he considered the most significant of his entire career, *On the Origin of the Knowledge of Right and Wrong*. A number of the pieces he published during this period had their origin in lectures that Brentano delivered to the "University of Vienna Philosophical Society," an organization he helped inspire and that was founded largely by his students in 1888.[11] According to the society's twenty-fifth anniversary publication, it was "in one of Franz Brentano's evening courses ... that quite independently from each other two listeners ... turned to (Alois) Höfler and asked whether they might not be able to gather on a voluntary but regular basis to discuss philosophical questions."[12] A fledgling

been subject to several years' thorough study...." Brentano's correspondence with Stumpf includes numerous undeniable references to "our direction" and other comparable phrases. Carl Stumpf, "Reminiscences of Franz Brentano," in *The Philosophy of Franz Brentano* (London: Duckworth & C., 1976), 10–45. One can better understand Brentano's antipathy to being called the head of a school when one considers that the notion of a "Brentano school" was often used by critics to describe the "scholastic" spirit of Brentano and his followers. See Alois Höfler, "Franz Brentano in Wien," in *Süddeutsche Monatshefte* (May 1917): 319–25.

11 Since Brentano was only a lecturer at the time, he was restricted to giving intellectual and moral support to the group. Material support for the Society came from Professor Robert Zimmerman. For more on the society, see Denis Fisette, "Austrian Philosophy and Its Institutions: Remarks on the Philosophical Society of the University of Vienna (1888–1938)," in *Mind, Values, and Metaphysics. Philosophical Essays in Honor of Kevin Mulligan*, volume 1 (London: Springer, 2014).

12 Quoted in John Blackmore, "Franz Brentano and the University of Vienna Philosophical Society 1888–1938," in *The Brentano Puzzle* (Farnham: Ashgate, 1998), 73–91.

group met regularly at the *Café Kaiserhof,* and then convened formally for the first time on February 21, 1888, in a lecture hall at the university. Brentano himself gave six lectures to the group and, according to John Blackmore, the period between 1888 and 1894 might rightly be dubbed the "Brentano period" since it was dominated by his students. During this period, as Blackmore observes, "it was widely believed that philosophy in so far as it was not dead was evolving into the science of psychology" and so "this meant … that lectures on psychology and physiology seemed to predominate." In this way, "[t]he Society was determined to save philosophy by making it scientific."[13]

Brentano's mission to rejuvenate philosophy did not stop him from starting a family. In a letter to Schell from December 1885, Brentano summarized the events leading to his decision to marry. Feeling somewhat lonely, he describes how he initially tried to have his sister Claudine to leave the convent and join him in Vienna.[14] Given his state of apostasy, Brentano was not insensitive to the possibility that the request might be rejected, and so he gave assurances to Church officials that he would in no way try to dissuade her from her Catholicism or influence her with his "freethinking." He even seemed to think that the arrangement would prevent the kind of outcry that might arise should he choose to marry, suggesting that he was already fully aware of the potential consequences of such an action. Austrian law forbade former priests from marrying, and even though Brentano was no longer a priest, he was acutely aware of continuing hostility towards him in Catholic circles. At any rate, the plan failed, and in September 1880, he married Ida von Lieben, daughter of the prominent businessman and banker Ignatz von Lieben and his wife Elise. The Liebens were related by marriage to the Gomperz and Todesco families, and "[t]aken together, the family and its relations constituted a veritable hub of capital, industry,

13 Blackmore, 77.

14 In the letter to Schell, Brentano describes feeling responsible for her being in Holy Orders, citing the example of his earlier religious devotion as a potential factor in her decision to enter the convent. See Schell, *Wegbereiter,* 44. The episode was also frustrating, since, as he wrote to his cousin Georg von Hertling, the request was denied without Brentano even being allowed to speak with his sister. The unpublished, undated letter is found in the Houghton Library Archive at Harvard University (bMs 216).

science and art."[15] Ida's siblings were all prominent members of Viennese society and included Leopold, president of the Vienna Stock Exchange, Helene, who married industrialist and member of parliament Rudolf Auspitz, the banker and economist Richard, and chemist and university professor Adolf. It was the latter who introduced Franz to Ida, and the couple were frequent guests in his home over the next decade. Although there is almost no record of the details of their courtship, evidence suggests that theirs was a happy union. His correspondence includes the expected, but not insincere, references to his "*aller-liebstes Frauchen*," tender references to their son Gio, and expressions of concern for Ida's health. Given the overwhelming professional orientation of most of Brentano's correspondence, limited mention of his domestic life is not surprising. But there are some other details that help illuminate the depth of their mutual commitment. In the summer of 1886, Edmund Husserl visited with the Brentano family in St. Gilgen, where Brentano and his wife together painted a portrait of Husserl.[16] There is also the moving account Brentano gives of Ida's last meeting with their son, his deep admiration for her concern that Gio not get sick because of her, and her concern that Brentano remarry so that their son not be raised by a stranger.[17]

But perhaps the best measure of Brentano's devotion to his wife might be the fact that he gave up his professorship to marry her, knowing that this move complicated his much valued professorship. Brentano gives different accounts of this decision. In a letter to Schell written in 1885, Brentano recalled knowing that this was a dangerous course of action:

> Our laws are so unclear and judicial interpretation so unreliable that, before I took the step, I asked for a clarification from the Ministry, whether they considered my actions legal. Admittedly, I knew the timing of the decision was poor. The minister

15 Karlheinz Rossbacher, *Literatur und Liberalismus* (Dachs, 1992), 60.
16 According to Husserl, "he would make improvements or even completely take over her pictures in progress, although it is true that she then had to lend a helping hand and do some things over again correctly." Edmund Husserl, "Reminiscences of Brentano," in *The Philosophy of Brentano* (London: Duckworth & Co., 1976), 53.
17 Schell, *Wegbereiter*, op. cit., 77.

himself advised me not to ask such questions, but just go ahead and marry. But I wanted everything to be above board, no matter what the cost. And so I opened the door for a negative response to my official inquiry. And so I gave up my professorship, acquired citizenship in Leipzig and even considered submitting my habilitation there. It pained me, of course, to think that, just like in Würzburg, everything in Vienna would also collapse after my departure. And so I first submitted my application for immediate habilitation in Vienna. Almost no one believed that it would be accepted, but the emperor and minister approved it, and in the following semester I stood once again before the podium as a lecturer.[18]

In this letter, Brentano states that he was not given assurances before he resigned that his professorship would be restored, which contradicts the claim he makes in *My Last Wishes for Austria* (published ten years later) that such assurances had been given to him. In the above account, he married knowing he had very little hope of having his habilitation accepted, much less having his professorship restored.[19] Of course, this letter was written five years after the event, and Brentano might have chosen to give a different version of events for one reason or another. But it is significant that in a letter to Stumpf from October 1880, Brentano never mentions having been assured of regaining his professorship: "And so, I am once again a lecturer, and held my first lecture today to great applause from the audience. The *capitis dimutio* does not make me unhappy. The increase in my happiness through greater goods than those that I have given up makes it entirely impossible to feel the misfortune." Would he call his situation a "misfortune" (*Übel*) if he was anticipating a restoration of his position based on promises already made? Possibly. There is no denying the light-hearted tone of the

18 Ibid., 46.
19 This contradicts those, like Alois Höfler, who claim that Brentano was blithely convinced he would regain his professorship "after a couple of weeks." See Höfler, "Franz Brentano in Wien," Brentano casts doubt on the trustworthiness of Höfler's account of his character in a letter to Hugo Bergmann. See Hugo Bergmann and Franz Brentano, "Briefe Franz Brentanos an Hugo Bergmann," in *Philosophy and Phenomenological Research* 7:1 (1946): 83–158.

letter, in which Brentano compares himself to Lazarus and goes on to discuss trivial things, like the fact that he and Ida have yet to find an apartment of their own, and closes with: "You see, I am in good humor, and write the usual nonsense."[20] The restoration of his professorship never materialized, of course, and this was a painful and frustrating fact for Brentano, but even as late as 1887, Brentano could write to Stumpf with a certain detachment: "God put me there and I won't leave my post. What do I care about the Minister and the Emperor, from whom I do not derive my mandate?"[21] Brentano's equanimity in these passages contrasts with his later ire over the situation. In his *My Last Wishes for Austria*, published in 1895, Brentano expressed frustration over the "chicanery" and "unpleasantness" surrounding his decision to marry, and gives a slightly different version of events than the one he gave to Schell. Describing how as a lecturer he had attracted an unprecedented number of students over the course of fourteen years, he declared: "Of course, I did it in the certain and unqualified conviction that new contributions for the university would give me the foundation to make a new claim on being made a full professor. (Otherwise, my sacrifice would have, in a certain sense, been a suicidal act.)"[22] One infers from this passage that he had been assured of having his professorship restored, but it is not something he states explicitly. It is therefore unclear, at least based on these sources, whether Brentano was given promises before he resigned. The point here is not to "catch" Brentano in a contradiction, or anything so petty. The point, rather, is to suggest the fact that Brentano did—pardon the cliché—risk everything for love.

Brentano and Ida von Lieben

And by "everything" I mean more than just his professional status. Marrying Ida thrust Brentano into a situation that was much more complicated, involving deeply fraught social and cultural issues, not the least of which was the fact that he was an ex-priest and a high-profile apostate marrying

20 Brentano, Goller, and Oberkofler, *Briefe an Carl Stumpf*, op. cit., 76.
21 Ibid., 90.
22 Franz Clemens Brentano, *Meine letzten Wünsche für Österreich* (J.G. Cotta, 1895), 12–13.

a Jewish woman. This was not a common occurrence. The Austrian Civil Code did not permit civil marriage, and only recognized marriages officiated by religious authorities. It did not, therefore, recognize marriage between members of different religious groups, unless approved by the relevant religious authorities. For a Jew to marry a Christian, therefore, they had to convert to Christianity, or both partners had to declare themselves "without confession." Not many did so. Between 1868 and 1903, 9000 Viennese Jews converted. About half of those converted to Catholicism. One quarter converted to Protestantism, and the other quarter declared themselves to be "without confession."[23] Marriages between persons "without confession" was thus far less common than marriages involving converted Jews, and were perhaps even more likely to attract attention as a result. Brentano was not unaware that his marriage attracted a lot of attention. As he noted in a letter to Schell: "I can, of course, imagine how strange it must affect a person raised according to Catholic habits to see [a former priest] engage in such a natural act [as marriage]. He finds it perfectly natural when a Jew, after baptism, no longer abides by the Mosaic dietary laws. But when a former priest leaves the Church and no longer cares about papal decrees— that must be a violation of his conscience."[24]

The reference here to a "person raised according to Catholic habits" is significant. Franz knew well the attitude he was describing. It may very well have been an attitude he himself shared early in his life, given his upbringing. What is certain is that it is an attitude he had to deal with regularly since leaving the priesthood and the Church. Even later in life people continued to write and tell him they prayed for his return to the Church.[25] But above all, the characterization here befitted Franz's mother, who was pained deeply by his apostasy, though she did her best to maintain cordial relations with her son and took care not to make things more difficult for him. This is clear in letters to several of her children, in which she voiced her disapproval of his decision and her hope that God will lead him back to the

23 These statistics are found in Rider, *Modernity and Crises of Identity*, 187. For more general information on conversions, see Todd Endelman, *Leaving the Jewish Fold: Conversion and Radical Assimilation in Modern Jewish History* (Princeton University Press, 2015).
24 Schell, *Wegbereiter*, op. cit., 45.
25 Ibid., 62.

Church and to the priesthood. Though she wrote that she had nothing against Ida personally, she considered a meeting with her "impossible."[26] The reference to Jews who leave the faith is also significant. The Liebens were a prominent, assimilated Jewish family, and according to Franz, Ida shared his general views regarding religion. She was not, as is sometimes reported, baptized, but declared herself officially "without confession" (*konfessionslos*) in order to marry.[27] She was thus, in an important way, the real, living counterpart of the Jew Brentano described in the letter to Schell. He was therefore well-positioned to see first-hand how Jews reacted to those who left their religion, and to compare the relative reaction of Catholics and Jews. The comparison is therefore far from abstract or offhand, but very much rooted in his experience standing at the intersection of these two communities. As we shall see, it was not the only time he drew on this experience to make this kind of comparison.

Brentano's connection to the assimilated Viennese Jewish community is more significant than has been heretofore considered.[28] Franz and Ida

26 Brigitte Schad, *Die Aschaffenburger Brentanos: Beiträge zur Geschichte der Familie aus unbekanntem Nachlass-Material* (Geschichts und Kunstverein Aschaffenburg, 1984), 84.

27 William Johnston claims that Ida was "a baptized Jewish patrician." See Johnston, *The Austrian Mind*, 291. This fact is contradicted by her niece, Josefine Winter, who confirms that she "did not convert to Christianity out of pious respect for her parents, but instead became 'without confession.'" See Winter, *Fünfzig Jahre eines Wiener Hauses*, op. cit., 12. It should be noted that Johnston is also mistaken in his assertion that Brentano "embodied the values of Bohemian Reform Catholicism."

28 For all their interest in fin-de-siècle Vienna over the last few decades, historians have paid little attention to Brentano except to offer boilerplate summaries of his influence on figures such as Freud and Husserl. Among the more prominent historical works to refer to Brentano in this way are: Carl E. Schorske, *Fin-de-Siècle Vienna: Politics and Culture* (CUP Archive, 1981); Allan Janik, Stephen Toulmin, and Stephen Edelston Toulmin, *Wittgenstein's Vienna* (Ivan R. Dee Publisher, 1996); Johnston, *The Austrian Mind*; Robert Weldon Whalen, *Sacred Spring: God and the Birth of Modernism in Fin de Siècle Vienna* (Eerdmans Publishing, 2007). The exception is Michael Steinberg, who has suggested that Brentano was "the single figure through which the intellectual culture of Musil, Freud, and Wittgenstein can be refracted. He is the person who defined the intellectual culture of the Austrian fin-de-

lived their entire married life together in an apartment on the third floor of a house at Oppolzergasse 6, on Vienna's *Ringstrasse* next to the *Burgtheater* just above the renowned *Café Landtmann*. They shared the house with Ida's brother Leopold and his wife Anna, and with her sister Helene and her husband Rudolf Auspitz, who bought the house in 1872. Diagnosed with severe depression, Helene was committed to an asylum in 1879, and both Ida and Franz lent a frequent hand raising and educating the Auspitz children. According to Josefine Winter, Helene's daughter, Brentano "doted most affectionately on his nieces and nephews, and played a decisive role in the life of the family."[29] She recalls how

> [i]t was the first time that a Christian (let alone a former Catholic priest) married into a Jewish family that, while enlightened, still maintained a sense of piety. To be sure, there were at first certain reservations regarding this union, no matter how freethinking the Liebens were. But how could one resist Franz Brentano's fascinating personality, with its combination of the dark handsomeness of an Apostle with a deep broad education, refined artistic taste, multiple talents, and a rock solid character! One had already to fall in love with the soft, resonant voice. But it was precisely the lack of prejudice on his part with which he met the Jewish family and valued the people without

siècle in terms of ambivalences." See Michael P. Steinberg, "'Fin-de-Siècle Vienna' Ten Years Later: 'Viel Traum, Wenig Wirklichkeit,'" in *Austrian History Yearbook* 22 (1991): 151–62. The only serious mention of Brentano's relationship to Jews is in Rossbacher, *Literatur und Liberalismus*. Among philosophers, Wilhelm Baumgartner has offered the most extensive analysis of Brentano's Viennese context, and shows how his relationship to Austria was structured in advance by factors such as his Catholic background and other sociocultural factors. Baumgartner notes that Brentano felt very much at home with his wife's family and their extended network, including the Gomperz, Ausptiz, Wertheimstein, and Todesco families, but does not comment on their leading role among assimilated Jewish families. See Wilhelm Baumgartner, "Brentano und die Österreichische Philosophie," in *Phenomenology and Analysis. Essays in Central European Philosophy* (Frankfurt: Ontos, 2004).

29 Josefine Winter, *Fünfzig Jahre eines Wiener Hauses* (Braumüller, 1927), 13.

consideration of heritage or belief that bode well for Ida's happiness.[30]

According to Winter, "*Onkel Franz*" was always coming down to the second floor and joining in the children's games. He was especially keen to share his passion for chess with them, and they all marveled at how he fashioned his own chess figures out of lead. But he was equally interested to share new games like Boccia, which he brought back from a trip to Italy, and the boomerang. Once he even built them a water carousel (*Wasserkarussell*). He also invited them to observe simple scientific experiments and enjoyed riddles and word play. He was also musical, and the children enjoyed hearing the sound of the piano from the third floor. "But the best and most precious thing that Uncle Franz bestowed on the group of children ... were the recitation evenings when all of the nieces and nephews gathered every Thursday in the winter years between 1886 and 1889."[31] In the five-sided room he used as a study, by the light of a single lamp with a green shade, Brentano read the children fairy tales (some from his uncle Clemens), poems, and longer adventure tales. Later, he read them Shakespeare, Cervantes, and of course Goethe. They finished the evenings "with pineapple bread or other similar delicacies prepared by Aunt Ida."[32]

This portrait of Brentano as a beacon of culture for the Lieben children is especially significant given that it took place on Vienna's famed *Ringstraße*.[33] Constructed between 1858 and 1865 to replace the city's old fortifications, Vienna's *Ringstraße* was more than an effort at modernization

---

30 Ibid.

31 Ibid., 22.

32 Karlheinz Rossbacher gives a starkly different interpretation of these evenings. He criticizes the repeated reading of Clemens Brentano's "Gockel, Hinkel, und Gackeleia," which featured stock anti-Semitic Jewish stereotypes, to Jewish children "as though this were nothing to these families." See Rossbacher, *Literatur und Liberalismus*, 289.

33 This portrait is only enhanced by the image given by Max Foges, who describes how lectures with Brentano didn't end, but continued out into the *Ringstraße*. Max Foges, "Persönliche Erinnerungen an F. Brentano," in *Neues Wiener Journal* (March 1917).

and the construction of a thoroughfare around the heart of the old city. It was "an open-air museum of artistic heritage for the edification of all peoples."[34] The *Ringstraße* featured monumental public buildings such as the university, city hall, the new palace, the opera, and multiple theaters and museums, whose individual architectural styles, as Carl Schorske has argued, served a distinctly "symbolic function of representation."[35] But more importantly, the *Ringstraße* represented the aspirations of the Viennese liberal-bourgeoisie at the height of their self-confidence in the third quarter of the century. It was during this period—beginning after the defeat against Italy at in 1859 and ending with the stock market crash of 1873—that the liberal bourgeoisie sought to reform Austrian society and politics in its image, championing constitutional reform, education, urban moderniza-tion, rights for different national groups, fiscal reform, and a restriction of clerical influence. Their "cultural self-projection" onto the *Ringstraße* meant that its avenues and boulevards served as a veritable theatre for staging the hopes and dreams of the Austrian bourgeoisie. That Franz and Ida—a free-thinking ex-Catholic priest married to an assimilated Jew—lived promi-nently on the *Ringstraße* can likewise be interpreted *à la Schorske* as a symbolic challenge to an outdated *status quo* and a desire for the transition to a more liberal political culture. To be sure, Brentano was no political lib-eral; indeed liberals feared Brentano's arrival in Vienna as much as Catholics.[36] According to Emil Utitz, Brentano actually "tended towards a certain political nihilism," evidence for which includes a short poem he was fond of quoting whose opening stanza was: *Weh! Wer dem Staat weihet seine Kraft/Wo jeden hemmt das vielverschlungene Streben/Heil, wer sich müht um Kunst und Wissenschaft/Wo jeder jeden tragen hilft und heben.*[37] But far from excluding him from the liberal-bourgeoisie, Brentano's aversion to poli-tics—his "political nihilism"—placed him squarely inside of a distinct seg-ment of this class, the *Bildungsbürgertum*. As any student of German culture and politics knows, the *Bildungsbürgertum* was a segment of the larger

34 Jacques Le Rider, *Modernity and Crises of Identity: Culture and Society in Fin-de-Siècle Vienna* (Continuum, 1993), 191.
35 Schorske, *Fin-de-Siècle Vienna*, op. cit., 26.
36 Schell, *Wegbereiter*, op. cit., 85.
37 Emil Utitz, "Erinnerungen an Franz Brentano," *Wissenschaftliche Zeitschrift Der Martin-Luther Universität* 4:1 (December 28, 1954): 86–87.

liberal-bourgeoisie who defined itself by its cultural aspirations, and by elevating these above active political engagement.[38] "Though liberals in the usual sense" might "never have been [his] friends," as he himself noted, this does not mean he should not be counted among those who aspired to a more broadly liberal culture or politics.[39] His stress on the natural sciences, his critique of religion, and his dedication to the ideals of culture—so lovingly described by his niece, who credited him with introducing her and her siblings to "the beautiful and the good"[40]—all testify to Brentano's abiding conviction that *Bildung* (self-formation) was the highest attainable good, a conviction that aligned him with the deepest values of the liberal-bourgeoisie.

They also aligned him with Viennese Jews who also saw culture as a vehicle of assimilation, a community that, perhaps more than any other, welcomed him and gave him a home. It has yet to be sufficiently appreciated the degree to which Brentano's life was bound together with the fate of Jewish members of the liberal-bourgeoisie; that is to say, with those who sought, through art, science, and culture, to complete and fulfil the promise of emancipation. Like them, he was convinced that science and culture were instruments for recasting the very foundations of society. He was also, like them, deeply skeptical of religion, at least as a set of form principles and practices codified in institutions. A deeply committed theist, Brentano considered religion a surrogate for true wisdom, and was sharply critical of the historical

38 The classic outline of this "non-political" posture remains Thomas Mann, *Reflections of a Nonpolitical Man* (Ungar, 1987).
39 Schell, *Wegbereiter*, op. cit., 85. That Brentano eludes easy classification is well known. He was not a political liberal, yet characterizations of him as a conservative Christian fail too. He was indelibly marked by his early devotion to Catholicism, but his deep criticism of the Church and Christianity make it impossible to put him squarely in this camp. For more on his early life and influences, especially from the perspective of Catholic intellectual history, see Dieter Münch, "Franz Brentano und die katholische Aristoteles-Rezeption im 19 Jahrhundert," in *Phenomenology and Analysis: Essays on Central European Philosophy*, eds., Arkadiusz Chrudzimski and Wolfgang Huemer (Ontos, 2004), 159–98. Richard Schaefer, "Infallibility and Intentionality: Franz Brentano's Diagnosis of German Catholicism," in *Journal of the History of Ideas* 68: 3 (2007): 477–99.
40 Winter, *Fünfzig Jahre eines Wiener Hauses*, op. cit., 25.

religions and their strictures on orthodoxy. He would thus have shared with these assimilated Jews a view of progress measured in terms directly relatable to the Jewish experience; that is to say, how key benchmarks in the integration of Jews—emancipation, tolerance, assimilation, intermarriage—were more broadly indicative of historical and social progress. He would also no doubt have been keenly aware of the growing anti-Semitism in Viennese culture and politics that began taking hold in the mid-1870s, and how this frustrated liberal Jewish aspirations.[41] Just how rising anti-Semitism clashed with the hopes of an earlier liberal faith can be illustrated, of course, with reference to Sigmund Freud. As Carl Schorske has shown, Freud and other assimilated Jews of his generation were much more skeptical than their parents' generation that liberalism could reconcile the national, political, religious, and other difficulties besetting the empire. They knew only too well how many barriers continued to stand in the way of their personal and professional self-realization. In his autobiography, Freud describes how his faith in liberal politics was shaken by his confrontation with anti-Semitism: "When, in 1873, I first joined the University, I experienced some appreciable disappointment. Above all, I found I was expected to feel myself inferior and an alien because I was a Jew."[42]

Given the realities of anti-Semitism, Freud (like so many others) found himself increasingly alienated from the liberal hopes of his father, who adorned the family home with pictures of liberal ministers. Against this backdrop, Schorske interprets Freud's discovery of psychoanalysis as a "political theory, the central principle of which is that all politics is reducible to the primal conflict between father and son."[43] In a brilliant reading of *The Interpretation of Dreams*, Schorske points to Freud's conflict with his

41 The collapse of the economy in 1873, and the associated scandals surrounding people like Ritter von Ofenheim, is usually seen as the beginning of the decline for Austrian liberals and the rise of anti-Semitism. By the late 1870s, anti-Semitism had made steady inroads into Viennese society. Georg von Schönerer and his pan-German party and Karl Lueger's Christian Social Party were active since the 1880s, and anti-Semitism was certainly a significant force at the university, especially in student fraternities such as "Teutonia" and "Libertas." See Rider, *Modernity and Crises of Identity*, op. cit., 197.

42 Quoted in Rider, *Modernity and Crises of Identity*, op. cit., 209.

43 Schorske, *Fin-de-Siècle Vienna*, op. cit., 197.

father as the generative context for the evolution of psychoanalysis, drawing on Freud's self-analysis of certain dreams to paint a compelling portrait of his frustration with a failed liberal politics. He shows how Freud's disappointment at his father's weakness in the face of anti-Semitism was the impetus for fantasies of resistance, triggered by a "Rome neurosis." Like so many nineteenth-century *bourgeois*, Freud was steeped in the history and culture of ancient Greece and Rome. In his reading of Freud's dreams, Schorske shows how Rome figures as a particularly fraught site of the interaction between Christian and Jewish symbolism that yields insight into Freud's longing for a way to overcome the various barriers to personal and professional self-fulfillment. In contrast with his own father, who did nothing to protest the humiliation of anti-Semitism, Freud fantasized about how the general Hannibal required his son to swear that he would avenge himself against the Romans. This dream, Schorske interprets as

> both pledge and project. And as project it was at once political and filial. In most of the other great creative Viennese who were Freud's contemporaries, the generational revolt against the fathers took the specific historical form of rejection of their fathers' liberal creed.... Not so Freud, at least not consciously. He defined his oedipal stance in such a way as to overcome his father by realizing the liberal creed his father professed but had failed to defend. Freud-Hannibal as "Semitic general" would avenge his feeble father against Rome, a Rome that symbolized "the organization of the Catholic Church" and the Habsburg regime that supported it.[44]

For Schorske, Freud's discovery of psychoanalysis was thus a "counterpolitical triumph" that displaced political disappointment from the realm of history into the realm of an eternal and primal struggle between fathers and sons. In this way, Freud gave his fellow liberals an "a-historical theory of man and society that could make bearable a political world spun out of orbit and beyond control."[45]

The close connection between Brentano and Freud has long been

44 Ibid., 191.
45 Ibid., 203.

acknowledged.[46] Freud attended Brentano's lectures, and joined other students in the famous weekly philosophical discussions in the Oppolzergasse.[47] And Brentano, for his part, recommended Freud to Theodor Gomperz for the job of translating John Stuart Mill. He was also apparently very supportive in helping Freud achieve his onetime goal of being a dual major in philosophy and zoology. Though Freud did not pursue a degree in philosophy, the two men would certainly have continued to see each other, especially during the period between 1888 and 1893 when Freud treated Brentano's sister-in-law, Anna von Lieben, for hysteria.[48] During that period, Freud visited the house as much as twice a day, administering morphine, and perfecting his "cathartic" method of analysis. Peter Swales has shown how Anna von Lieben was in fact the "Frau Cäcilie M." who, in Studies in Hysteria, Freud credited with being his "teacher." He further describes how Freud was someone the Lieben children "feared and detested—for them he was 'der Zauberer,' the magician come to put their mother into a trance yet again and to accompany her through her fits of ravings, screamings, and long declamatory speeches." As Jill Lloyd observes, "from the family's point of view, there was a darker side to Freud's visits, only hinted at in his published notes. For some time, Anna had been addicted to morphine, and Freud's visits were also to supervise her daily injections of the drug.... Watching these daily events, the children regarded Freud with suspicion, believing that he was doing their mother more harm than good; they actually thought that the man with the black beard who passed

46 James Ralph Barclay, "Franz Brentano and Sigmund Freud," in *Journal of Existentialism* 5 (1964): 1–33; Günter Gödde, "Freuds Philosophische Diskussionskreise in Der Studentenzeit," in *Jahrbuch Der Psychoanalyse* 27 (1991): 73–113; William J. McGrath, *Freud's Discovery of Psychoanalysis: The Politics of Hysteria* (Cornell University Press, 1986).

47 Husserl paints a particularly warm picture of these discussions, and Brentano's devotion to his students. See Husserl, "Reminiscences of Brentano," op. cit., 48.

48 In a letter from the period Ida reports: "On account of the illness of my sister-in-law Lieben ... I rush back and forth like a pendulum and get nothing else done." Quoted in Peter J. Swales, "Freud, His Teacher and the Birth of Psychoanalysis," in *Freud: Appraisals and Reappraisals* (Hillsdale, N.J.: The Analytic Press, 1986), 25.

through their nursery on his way to alleviate Anna's most recent crisis was a magician rather than a doctor."[49]

But just exactly how deep an impression Brentano made on Freud has only relatively recently come to light. In his *Freud's Discovery of Psychoanalysis*, William McGrath explores Freud's correspondence with his friend Eduard Silberstein, which reveals just how enamored Freud was of his philosophy teacher, whom he described in one letter as: "this remarkable man and in many respects ideal human being (he is a believer in God, a teleologist!) and Darwinian and a damned clever fellow, indeed one of genius."[50] Freud was particularly impressed by Brentano's arguments on behalf of the existence of God, which he made in a dispassionate way that clearly unsettled Freud's view of the antipathy between religion and science. Writing to Silberstein, Freud observed (not entirely uncritically) that Brentano "is a man who came here to found schools and win followers and who thus directs his warmth and friendliness to anyone who asks something of him. I have not, however, been able to escape his influence. I am not capable of disproving a simple theistic argument which forms the crown of his expositions.... He proves to me the existence of God with as little partiality and as much exactitude as someone else might present the advantages of the wave over the particle theory."[51] Clearly, the scientific thrust of Brentano's proof troubled Freud, who reported being "afraid of being captured by ... spiritualism, homeopathy, Louise Lateau, and so forth."[52] That such a deeply divisive and politically sensitive issue as religion could be addressed in such a way was nothing short of revelatory to the young Freud, who in one letter sounds like a committed Brentanian: "For you must make no mistake about it, the existence of God is not to be resolved through society debates or parliamentary speeches nor through speculative thought, but only through logical and psychological investigations."[53]

---

49   Jill Lloyd, *The Undiscovered Expressionist: A Life of Marie-Louise Von Motesiczky* (Yale University Press, 2007), 15.

50   William J. McGrath, *Freud's Discovery of Psychoanalysis: The Politics of Hysteria*, 112.

51   Ibid., 116.

52   Ibid., 188.

53   Ibid., 120.

Brentano's "Last Wishes" for Austria

If Schorske is right, and the Viennese Jews who came of age in the fourth quarter of the century channeled unresolved disappointment in their fathers into scientific and aesthetic pursuits, then to what extent might it be fair to read Brentano as a lodestar for precisely this generation? As McGrath observes, "Freud's Hannibal phantasy would certainly have predisposed him to admire a man who had first defied the pope in resigning from the priesthood and had then defied both emperor and cardinal in accepting the Vienna position."[54] Viewed in this light, might Brentano have been something of a substitute father figure, not in a strictly psychological sense, but in a cultural one? Given the obvious effect he had on Freud, at least for a time, might we not see Brentano as a particularly attractive figure for Viennese Jews who, disappointed in the failure of liberalism, longed for a path to conquering "Rome"? This line of thinking reminds us that it was assimilated Viennese Jews who were perhaps the most sympathetic to Brentano's fight to have his marriage recognized and his professorship restored, and who was perhaps the most unambiguously supportive audience for his very public commentary on the state of Austrian society, *My Last Wishes for Austria*.

Consisting of a series of newspaper articles first published in December 1894 in *Neue Freie Presse*, along with critical responses from *Das Vaterland* and Brentano's rejoinders, the volume was published in 1895. In it, Brentano summarized his interactions with various government officials, pointing to instances when he had been reassured of reappointment to a professorship, only to be subsequently and repeatedly disappointed. He summarized his efforts to justify such a reappointment, pointing to his large class sizes and his efforts aimed at rejuvenating philosophy along empirical lines. He also repeated his call for the creation of an institute for psychology as a way for Vienna to stay at the forefront of scientific progress. But he also went beyond chronicling his personal circumstances to offer final "hopes" for Austria. First, he hoped that the state would "learn to be grateful for loyal service."[55] Second, he hoped that the example of his legal battle and the intolerance he suffered would motivate reform so that others would

54 Ibid., 111.
55 Brentano, *Meine letzten Wünsche*, op. cit., 10.

not have to suffer his fate. And finally, he hoped that Austria would cultivate a deeper devotion to science, and have the courage to stop those who would politicize science for narrow ends. He also made a passionate plea for peace among the various national groups: "May Austria find its inner peace! May its people of different nationalities not forget the unity of their culture, and may they transform their squabble over relatively small matters into a competition over who can best promote the highest welfare of all."[56]

The bulk of *My Last Wishes for Austria* focuses on the legal issues surrounding Brentano's bid to be reinstated as a full professor. The central issue turned on the legal interpretation of paragraph 63 of the Austrian Civil Code, which stated that "clergy ordained in the higher orders, as well as those lower clergy of both sexes who have given a solemn oath to remain celibate cannot enter into a legal marriage."[57] Brentano argued that the state, both in principle and in point of fact, recognized the legality of people who changed confession or who became "without confession." It was absurd therefore to hold that those who had taken Holy Orders were still bound by their oath once they had formally left the priesthood (let alone, in his case, the Church). As evidence, he cited the case of the former priest Franz Pawlovsky, whose conversion to Protestantism was recognized by the Prague court as sufficient for him to enter into a legal marriage. In support of his position, Brentano drew on the legal opinions of Julius Glaser, former justice minister and liberal politician, and Joseph Unger, another prominent Viennese legal authority and politician.[58] His opponents held otherwise, stressing (with the Church) that an oath was not something that could be rescinded, since it was of a sacramental nature. They cited Eduard Rittner, who in his *Österreichisches Eherecht* argued that, in the matter of marriage, Austrian civil law was intended to replicate Church law without exception; indeed the civil law was based in whole on Church law. According to Rittner, the law admitted of no qualifications, not as a "matter of obligation

---

56 Ibid., 29.
57 Written in 1811, the Civil Code clashed with the provisions of the Austrian Constitution of 1867 guaranteeing religious freedom and confessional parity throughout the empire. The debate therefore turned on Supreme Court decisions interpreting how the law should be applied.
58 Both were also friends of the family.

to the Church, but as a limit of personal legal competence in the area of civil law."[59] This line of reasoning was echoed in an article published in *Das Vaterland* (included in Brentano's volume), in which the author argued that the determination of who is or is not still in Holy Orders is not a matter of individual caprice, but rather a matter for the Church to decide. It is not sufficient for someone to declare himself to be no longer a priest or a Catholic.[60] Brentano responded by arguing that there existed no law which stated that a person who had once taken Holy Orders was bound by them for life. But more importantly, this entire way of thinking suffered a major "fallacy" (*Trugschluss*). To follow Rittner would mean that it was entirely impossible for someone to leave the Church, and the state could never recognize conversion of any kind. The state would be beholden to enforce Canon law, and would have no legal room to recognize religious minorities, converts, or dissenters. This was absurd, however, given the fact that this class of persons was recognized by the state in myriad ways daily.[61] While the Church may—as is its prerogative—define its members according to sacraments that carry an "indelible" character, the state must safeguard the rights of those who have left the Church. This was not only consistent with practice and with the basic impetus behind the code of civil law, but was important for safeguarding morality and order. How could it serve public order to force unbelieving priests to remain celibate, when this in all likelihood would lead to "the coarsest moral disorder one can imagine?"[62]

History, Progress, and the New Christianity

Brentano reported having been encouraged to publish *My Last Wishes for Austria* by those who thought it might be of interest to future historians looking

59 Brentano, *Meine letzten Wünsche*, op. cit., 21.
60 Ibid., 51.
61 Brentano recounts the following humorous episode: "It is impossible that Herr Rittner can ignore that a former Christian and priest are no longer truly a Christian and a priest, since in a previous conversation with me, he understood that a former professor is no longer a professor. Moreover, in seeking an appropriate form of address, it certainly did not occur to him to address me at the time as your eminence." Ibid., 25.
62 Ibid., 27.

to understand Austria at the end of the century.[63] Certainly, the "Brentano case" (*Der Fall Brentano*) was well known in Vienna and beyond, reports of it appearing throughout German-speaking Europe in such varied journals as: *Akademische Revue, Die Nation, Die Grenzboten, Die Zeit, Hochschulnachrichten,* and *Evangelisches-Kirchenzeitung.* And yet, one wonders whether he wasn't also motivated by the fact that he knew there was a receptive audience among assimilated Viennese Jews eager to join him in his wholesale condemnation of the reactionary quality of recent Austrian politics.[64] It is all too easy while reading *My Last Wishes for Austria* to get caught up in the ethical and legal issues, and lose sight of the fact that Brentano was at that time no longer seeking to regain his professorship. This was not a call to redress a grievance. It was a parting shot against a system that had already failed, a broadside against the aging, decadent empire that Robert Musil famously characterized as *Kakania.*[65] It was a high-profile demand that the state protect its citizens from overweening clerical influence, and it is not hard to imagine how significant this fight would have been for beleaguered Viennese liberals. Brentano's unremitting defense of tolerance, religious freedom, and scientific progress were no doubt welcome balm to liberal readers who had seen their agenda overwhelmed by conservative forces over the course of the last quarter of the century. But there is another dimension to Brentano's text that deserves attention. In addition to a public judgment on the backward tendency of Austrian politics, this was a defense of his decidedly non-traditional marriage to a Jewish woman. This is not immediately evident. But it is important to bear in mind that Brentano wrote the piece less than a year after Ida's death, at a time when he was deciding whether or not to leave Vienna, and no doubt reflecting on their life together. He points to this himself in his opening paragraph in which he recalled:

63 He notes the same in Schell, *Wegbereiter*, op. cit., 59.
64 The fact that Brentano's original articles appeared in *Neue Freie Presse* is suggestive in this regard. Though not a "Jewish newspaper" in any clear sense, it was an important forum for "the Viennese Jewish establishment ... to defend its principles." Rider, *Modernity and Crises of Identity*, op. cit., 191.
65 Brentano's student Alois Höfler called it a "profanity (Fluch) against Austrian University-philosophy and politics." See Höfler, "Franz Brentano in Wien," op. cit., 325.

It has been twenty years since I've been attached to Austria, to Vienna and her University. I came with a warm, ancestral sympathy for the land and its people, and I was received with the warmest welcome. And when one of the noblest daughters of Vienna gave me her hand in marriage, I felt myself even more closely bound in brotherhood to my new countrymen. And yet it is precisely this that has become the occasion for me—insulted and oppressed on multiple occasions and stymied in my best intentions to serve the common good—to consider leaving Austria.[66]

What stands out here, of course, is the interweaving of Brentano's personal and professional happiness; his marriage is the occasion for a greater devotion to Austria but then becomes the impediment to him serving the greater good. This is especially important to note since there is almost no mention of his marriage throughout the remainder of the text, except in connection with technical legal issues. Compared with this opening declaration, the rest of the text seems coldly analytic. This shouldn't surprise us. Brentano's goal was to offer a dispassionate analysis of problems in the Austrian legal system and society more generally. But that should not prevent us from acknowledging—as Brentano himself did—how it was his marriage that was the cause of his troubles. And these were far from merely legal difficulties.[67] Brentano's marriage left him open to criticism from several different angles. There was the Catholic who could, and did, accuse him of violating the sacrament of Holy Orders. There was the Austrian who could, and did,

---

66 Brentano, *Meine letzten Wünsche*, op. cit., 9.

67 Gerald Stourzh calls attention to how important and controversial these marriages were in Vienna during the last decades of the century. Though very little research has been done on them, what is certain is that they were always complicated. In cases involving conversion, as Stourzh points out, "[T]hose who were 'converts' for one side were 'apostates' for the other side." This concern for apostasy was no less relevant for those who declared themselves "without confession," since leaving the fold could just as easily incur criticism as converting. Gerald Stourzh, *From Vienna to Chicago and Back: Essays on Intellectual History and Political Thought in Europe and America* (University of Chicago Press, 2010), 246.

accuse him of tepid loyalty, since he became (and remained) a Saxon in order to marry.[68] There were those who accused him of marrying for money, or of being unable to bear the burden of celibacy. [69] And there were also those who could accuse him of luring away a member of the Jewish faith. Brentano himself addressed this criticism in *My Last Wishes for Austria*, and cited Bavarian and Viennese newspapers as having started the rumor that he was committed to securing Jews for Christianity. It centered on the fact that, as a young man in his hometown in Aschaffenburg, Brentano played a role in converting a classmate, Franz Adler, from Judaism to Catholicism.[70] Brentano responded by explaining how, at the time, he merely gave a frank account of his sincere love for Christ and Catholicism to a friend who had asked. He was not motivated to convert him away from Judaism as such, and stated bluntly that "even then I didn't suffer from anti-Semitism."[71]

Regardless of the criticisms levelled against him, Brentano remained committed to staying above mud-slinging. Even when *Das Vaterland* referred derisively to Brentano's "so-called marriage," he barely acknowledged it. Instead, he remained focused on the bigger issues like the rights of conscience, protection for religious dissenters, an over-reaching Church, and the need to promote rigorous scientific thinking. These were, for Brentano, the earmarks of progress, and he was nothing if not devoted to the idea that history was subject to definite periods of progress and decline. Brentano was a deeply historical thinker. He was convinced that he and his students were on the

---

68 In his "reminiscences" of Franz Brentano, Husserl refutes both of these charges. See Husserl, "Reminiscences of Brentano."

69 Brentano also publicly denied that celibacy played any role in his decision. See Brentano, *Meine letzten Wünsche*, 28.

70 It should be noted that Adler and Brentano remained in touch, and their correspondence shows that Adler remained steadfast in his commitment to win Brentano back to the Church. Their unpublished correspondence is available at the *Forschungsstelle und Dokumentationszentrum für Österreichische Philosophie* in Graz. For more on Adler and his conversion, see Elias H. Füllenbach OP and Gianfranco Miletto, *Dominikaner und Juden / Dominicans and Jews: Personen, Konflikte und Perspektiven vom 13. bis zum 20. Jahrhundert / Personalities, Conflicts, and Perspectives from the 13th to the 20th Century* (Walter de Gruyter GmbH & Co KG, 2014).

71 Brentano, *Meine letzten Wünsche*, op. cit., 62.

vanguard of a new stage in the cycle of philosophical phases, and that this was a moment of consequence for the course of European culture more generally.[72] Viewed in this light, his departure from Vienna was therefore full of potential implications, not just for the state of philosophy, but for *fin-de-siècle* Austria itself. Brentano was explicit about this. The publication of *My Last Wishes for Austria* declared Austria moribund from the point of view of philosophy and its role in history. In the third of his original three articles he recounted his efforts to found an institute for experimental psychology, and described how these were largely ignored by the education ministry. Brentano concluded that, though the education ministry had been given its freedom by the constitution of 1867, this freedom was nevertheless still being thwarted at the administrative level. He cited the declaration by the Minister of Education Stanislas Madeyski, who held that, as the seat of the Apostolic Nuncio, Vienna had to be held to higher account in all matters, including education. Given that the minister's declaration was made in connection with developments in the philosophy department, Brentano responded:

> How could I not fear that, after my departure, everything would get off the right track? The danger of that happening is, in fact, imminent, for our time is a time of transition, of awakening for philosophy after a period of capricious, dreamlike constructions. The weeds have not yet all been pulled. It takes an expert eye to appreciate what is special in precious seeds.[73]

Brentano went on to decry the misguided ideas many people had about philosophy, and declared yet again what was his basic conviction: philosophy was a science like other sciences. It therefore had essentially the same method as all other sciences: the method of the natural sciences. Recognizing this fact and practicing philosophy along these lines was essential for philosophy to be relevant and speak to the broader scientific community:

72 Balázs M. Mezei and Barry Smith, *The Four Phases of Philosophy* (Rodopi, 1998); Josef M. Werle, *Franz Brentano und die Zukunft der Philosophie: Studien zur Wissenschaftsgeschichte und Wissenschaftssystematik im 19. Jahrhundert* (Rodopi, 1989).
73 Brentano, *Meine letzten Wünsche*, op. cit., 31.

Only in this way will it stay in contact with the other sciences, since none of the other areas of knowledge are sharply separated from our own. They all overlap with each other in some way. This method has prevailed in all periods when philosophy has been on the rise, and when forgotten, decline has been the necessary result. The scientific character of research collapsed. It is therefore with great concern that I look at the possibility that this will happen when I leave, if not right away, then in time.[74]

To prevent such a collapse, Brentano encouraged the education ministry to rethink his proposal to found an institute for experimental psychology, which he argued would act as a bulwark against decline. This paean to scientific philosophy will, of course, be familiar to anyone who has read Brentano. But what is more important for our purposes is how Brentano saw progress and decline in philosophy as essentially congruent with progress and decline in culture and society more generally.

Brentano's views on history were guided by his understanding of what constituted good scientific philosophy and what did not, but his view of history was not shaped by his reading of the history of philosophy alone. Multiple considerations influenced how he read the course of history, not the least of which was his particular view of the evolution of religion, and in this we see a clear parallel with Andrew Dickson White. Brentano distinguished between primitive religion and what he considered the more advanced forms of monotheism, Christianity being preeminent among these. Monotheistic religions, in his view, were advanced enough to be considered a surrogate form of knowledge. Intuitively correct in their theoretical drive to know the cause and character of all things, they fell short of pure theoretical knowledge by being too mired in dogma and revelation to be susceptible to rigorous empirical analysis. The true aspiration of religion was thus philosophy, and Brentano remained a committed theist on philosophical grounds; indeed his defense of the existence of God was one of the prized results of his philosophical research and was a topic of great fascination for his students. His apostasy was thus not just a personal rejection of Catholicism, but an event he interpreted as a historical threshold of sorts. Although Brentano was the

74   Ibid., 33.

last to impose his beliefs on anyone else—he usually counselled students to convert to Protestantism as the "religion of those lacking religion"—he nevertheless held a firm belief that philosophy led inevitably away from religion.[75] Brentano makes this plain in a series of letters to Hugo Bergmann written in 1907 in which he strongly encouraged the younger man to overcome his lingering loyalty to Judaism and convert so that he could more easily be hired at a university.[76] Dismissing Bergmann's loyalty to Judaism as a "stubborn attachment to the legacy of a barbaric age," Brentano was unsympathetic with Bergmann's desire to stand in solidarity with fellow Jews against the injustice of anti-Semitism. For Brentano, the important thing was to move forward, for "intolerance is not aimed against something new ushered in by the spirit of progress. Rather, it is rather the remainder of a bygone age that is held on to tenaciously according to a social inertia."[77] One should be loyal to the truth and to moving forward, and so he warned Bergmann: "Don't be under any illusions. The halo that can be bestowed on one without confession who would rather accept all the disadvantages rather than join this or that religious community cannot be bestowed on you because of your continued fidelity to an external affirmation of faith that has lost its meaning."[78]

Brentano's views on philosophical and religious progress were thus mutually reinforcing, and together served as a barometer of historical progress more generally. But if this seems a somewhat familiar vision of progress—civilizational upswing as the result of scientific achievement—I want to defamiliarize it by suggesting that Brentano's views were also informed by his experience with assimilated Viennese Jews, and his conviction that Christianity was following a similar historical trajectory as Judaism. Brentano clearly thought Jews much better able to understand those who gave up their religion, as he made clear in his comparison between Catholic and Jewish reactions to apostasy. This was, no doubt, partly related to his personal experience with his wife's family and friends. But it was also something

75 Endelman, *Leaving the Jewish Fold*, op. cit., 119.
76 Bergmann was under pressure from Stumpf and Marty as well. The episode is discussed in Guillaume Fréchette, "Bergman and Brentano," *Grazer Philosophische Studien* 67:1 (2004): 209–25.
77 Bergmann and Brentano, "Briefe Franz Brentanos an Hugo Bergmann," op. cit., 130.
78 Ibid., 103.

Brentano drew from his reading of history. Jews were, in his estimation, better able to give up their religion, given the historical event of Judaism's supersession by Christianity. Christians therefore would do well to learn from Jews just how to cross the threshold to a post-Christian theism. This was not something he wrote about or discussed in his lectures. But in June 1895, just as the furor over his *My Last Wishes for Austria* was reaching its peak, Brentano wrote a letter to Schell in which he outlined this idea in no uncertain terms. In an uncharacteristically candid venting of frustration, he called the Church to account and demanded: "And where is the Church? One is known by the company one keeps, and this is a sad testimony. I say here: know thyself. Is it worthy of those born from the martyrs who suffered Roman tyranny—those who built courageously on the strength of conscience and declaring themselves part of a kingdom not of this world—to always use the power of the state and tools of coercion to oppress the freedom of those who think differently?"[79] The fact that the Church relied on the state to ensure orthodoxy was a sign of "deep decadence," a sign of weakness and decline. It was therefore appropriate to consider the lessons of history, and for Brentano, this meant acknowledging that Christianity was now where Judaism had once been: "Christianity is, in my view, just as obsolete as the Mosaic religion was at the time of Christ. Hell, original sin, salvation of the select few over the many … yes and also the many dogmas, that are expressed more in words than in concepts…. [T]hey are all known to be contrary to moral impulses, on the one hand, and to logic on the other, and irreconcilable with healthy psychology."[80] His view of the mis-fit between classic religion and "healthy psychology" is especially important, because it

---

79 Schell, *Wegbereiter*, op. cit., 60. Schell was the author of a variety of texts that sought to reform and modernize Catholicism. He was roundly denounced by many in the Church and four of his books were listed on the Index. One of the reasons Brentano was uncharacteristically frank in these statements, therefore, stems from the fact that he was addressing one whom he believed was on the cusp of a similar crisis of faith that he had experienced. Brentano perhaps hoped that a frank characterization of the "facts" (as he saw them) might help his friend see that Catholicism was not capable of regeneration in the way that Schell believed. Brentano is explicit about this at a variety of points in their correspondence.

80 Ibid.

shows clearly the way Brentano envisioned the close interplay between philosophy, theism, and history. Though generally polite and respectful when discussing the Church—almost to a fault—there is no question that, in this letter, Brentano consigned Catholicism and Christianity to the dustbin of history.[81] But in this instance, he offered an image that would have been startling to most of his contemporaries, to say the least: Christians were the new Jews.

In so thinking, Brentano did not dismiss the significance of Christianity. On the contrary, he always maintained that Christianity was a singularly influential force in shaping the history of Europe, and its basic theoretical and moral impulses were good. Jesus remained for him perhaps the most sublime figure in history, and a conduit of revelation about the true foundations of morality and basis for a sincere love of God.[82] Like A. D. White, Brentano believed that he was living on the cusp of a transition whereby the sublimation of what is "truest" in Christianity would lay the foundation for a new, purer theism. In support of this claim, Brentano drew on the example of ancient Judaism: "Just as the body of the old man, the organism of the Church cannot be made youthful. But it can bear new fruit, just as Judaism bore Christianity. At the end of my lecture on the four phases of philosophy, I hinted at the character of this new entity that would be brought forth in this way, if only in general terms." Though it would take time, and no doubt experience many setbacks, Brentano joined with White in believing that "an evolution will come to pass" that was an expression of divine providence.[83] This evolution would preserve the best and truest impulses of Christianity, such as the notion of an afterlife and the insight that "many are called and few are chosen." About heaven, Brentano wrote Schell in a subsequent letter that he didn't see it as "a final, quiet, consummation, but rather as a progressive transformation, for which the idea of optimism alone suffices."[84] In this second letter Brentano again drew on the supersession of Judaism as a

81 Husserl is only one of the many students who attest to this fact. Husserl, "Reminiscences of Brentano," op. cit., 49.

82 Franz Clemens Brentano, *Die Lehre Jesu und ihre bleibende Bedeutung: mit einem Anhange: Kurze Darstellung der christlichen Glaubenslehre* (F. Meiner, 1922).

83 Schell, *Wegbereiter*, op. cit., 61.

84 Ibid., 63.

trope for diagnosing the state of Christianity. Citing a prayer he had written for his son, Brentano told Schell it "might help illustrate … the relationship and difference between my new Christianity and the old one, which it appears to me more and more to be taking on the role of a new Judaism."[85]

By employing supersession as a trope for explaining the movement of history, Brentano tapped into one of the theological mainstays of traditional Christian anti-Semitism, and this needs to be acknowledged.[86] But using it to call Christians the new Jews complicates any attempt to see Brentano as anti-Semitic after the fashion of Georg Schönerer or Karl Lueger. Brentano saw Judaism as an atavistic holdover of ancient religion, but he did not see it as threatening the political order, or Germandom in any of its various imagined incarnations. If anything, its primary purpose—given the mood and tenor of these particular letters—was to condemn Christians; to offer them a stark picture of their situation that was provocative to say the least. That Brentano drew on his intimate experience with assimilated Viennese Jews in order to formulate this idea is, to my mind, certain. In the context of the ascendant anti-Semitism of the last quarter of the century, it is perhaps tempting to think Brentano saw this as a strategy for hollowing out the Christian impetus behind so much anti-Judaism. But there is no evidence of that. These were relatively isolated statements made in confidence to a friend whose primary purpose was to illustrate his burgeoning idea of a new Christianity. They do not represent an in-depth analysis of the relationship between Judaism and early Christianity. But precisely insofar as they were incidental, they help us see how the Viennese milieu was ready to hand as a resource for how he thought about history and his place in it. Yet again, they show how Brentano was not a free-floating "mind" who philosophized in abstract terms. On the contrary, he was deeply concerned to read the signs of the times, and was convinced that his reading of the history of philosophy and of history more generally revealed patterns that one could use to interpret the course of events and shore up hope for the future.

85 Ibid.
86 David Nirenberg, *Anti-Judaism: The Western Tradition* (W. W. Norton & Company, 2013).

EPILOGUE
RELIGION AND HISTORY

Devotional activism alerts us to those instances where opponents in a debate might be more alike than different in how they go about fighting for their goals. Though these goals might be very different, even diametrically opposed, the means used to fight for them can share a deeper affinity. This might seem a simple point, but it is one that is easily overlooked if we allow secularization and its cognates to pre-form our approach to history by imagining a strict linear line of development driven forward by certain incontestable values of progress and rationality framed in very narrow terms. For on this view, those who *do* contest those values, or fall short of what they require, are not simply chided for failing to "get with" or accommodate to the times; they are summarily displaced from history as "backward," "barbaric," or "medieval," a move that effectively inures modernity to criticism from those thus exiled from time. In one way or another, the essays collected here have all taken as their point of departure that historical research should be more self-reflexively critical in its approach to religion. Above all, they put paid to the tendency to structure debates involving religion by placing the opponents in these debates in different time zones. The essays collected here have sought to show what happens when we no longer presume that religion is modernity's other, and when we make a concerted effort to avoid what the anthropologist Johannes Fabian calls the denial of "coevalness." The denial of coevalness consists in "distancing those who are observed from the Time of the observer," and naturalizing the time of the observer in such a way as to render the observed "not yet ready for civilization."[1] As a mechanism for categorizing and regulating modernity's others,

1   It is an essential part of the "persistent and systematic tendency to place the referent(s) of anthropology in a Time other than the present of the producer of anthropological discourse," and lies at the center of systems of colonial domination in the modern period. Though Fabian's concern is to show how this tendency plays a structuring role in anthropology, it is no less true that

the denial of coevalness is central to modern self-understanding and modern historiography. As Michel de Certeau so astutely observed: "A structure belonging to modern Western culture can doubtless be seen in this historiography: intelligibility is established through a relation with the other; it moves (or "progresses") by changing what it makes of its "other"—the Indian, the past, the people, the mad, the child, the Third World."[2]

Religion too has been an ineluctable component of this historiographical structure, but there is no doubt that its grip is loosening. When I began my career nearly thirty years ago, rank and file academics were largely indifferent to religion if not openly hostile to the idea that it was anything more than a holdover from premodern societies. That is no longer the case, as scholars from various disciplines have taken a decidedly new and critical approach to the normative presuppositions undergirding the secularization paradigm, including taking a harder look at how secularization is mutually imbricated in powerful assumptions about the course of history itself. One of the most compelling, if surprising developments in this context has been the turn to religion in the recent work of Jürgen Habermas. Largely dismissive of religion for most of his long and prolific career, Habermas, an atheist, surprised many when he began paying increasing attention to religion in the early part of the twenty-first century. In a series of essays and public encounters, including an exchange with then Cardinal Joseph Ratzinger, Habermas sounded a new note of appreciation for the distinctly theological heritage of critical social theory.[3] But he has also expressed appreciation for the *ongoing* potential of religion to inform, and even re-charge, debates in the public sphere, and hence play an important role in the success of deliberative democracy. Religions provide not only the

history, sociology, and related disciplines have all engaged in a similar denial of coevalness in the name of defining and distinguishing what is modern from what is not, and using this distinction as a weapon of subjugation. Johannes Fabian, *Time and the Other. How Anthropology Makes its Object* (New York: Columbia UP, 1983), 25–26.

2   Certeau, *The Practice of Everyday Life*, op. cit., 3.

3   Jürgen Habermas and Eduardo Mendieta, *Religion and Rationality: Essays on Reason, God and Modernity* (Cambridge, Mass.: MIT Press, 2002). See also the various essays included in Eduardo Mendieta, ed., *The Frankfurt School on Religion. Key Writings by the Major Thinkers* (New York: Routledge, 2005).

historical root of certain abiding philosophical and social ideals, they continue to nourish moral intuitions that frame how many people undertake social and political action.[4] But Habermas went even further, and conceded that the theory of secularization had become largely moribund. In a striking turnabout, one that surprised no small number of his supporters, he challenged "secular citizens [who] are convinced that religious traditions and religious communities are … archaic relics of pre-modern societies … to grasp their conflict with religious opinions as a reasonably expected disagreement." Instead of dismissing these opinions, or ruling them out in advance as atavistic, they should look for "morally convincing intuitions and reasons" in what their religious opponents say. Doing so would not just open up a perspective on how and why religious actors take various positions, but might help rejuvenate the emotive and moral quality of arguments on both sides.

Habermas is one of the most significant and influential social theorists of our time, and his belated recognition of religion's significance for social theory confirms that we are in a moment when it is possible to draw different lessons from, and about, religion in history.[5] Instead of imposing a singular vision of progress on history reflecting a dogmatic commitment to secularization, Habermas insists that "postmetaphysical thought is prepared to learn from religion." To be sure, he also insists that one remain "agnostic in the process" and observe a strict separation "between the certainties of faith, on the one hand, and validity claims that can be publicly criticized,

4   "Universalistic egalitarianism, from which sprang the ideals of freedom and a collective life in solidarity, the autonomous conduct of life and emancipation, the individual morality of conscience, human rights and democracy, is the direct legacy of the Judaic ethic of justice and the Christian ethic of love. This legacy, substantially unchanged, has been the object of a continual critical reappropriation and reinterpretation." Jürgen Habermas, "A Conversation about God and the World: Interview with Eduardo Mendieta," in *Religion and Rationality: Essays on Reason, God, and Modernity*, ed., Eduardo Mendieta (Cambridge, MA: MIT Press, 2005), 149.

5   For a good overview of the various steps leading Habermas to his interest in religion, see Eduardo Mendieta, "Religion in Habermas's Work," in *Habermas and Religion*, eds., Craig Calhoun, Eduardo Mendieta, and Jonathan Van Antwerpen (New York: Polity, 2013), 391–407.

on the other." But he is nevertheless unequivocal in his support for a "post-secular" approach that "refrains from the rationalist presumption that it can itself decide what part of the religious doctrines is rational and what part irrational. The contents which reason appropriates through translation must not be lost for faith."[6] Taking a post-secular approach means abjuring the impulse to write religion out of modern history, and embracing the possibility that one might learn certain things from religious sources that had been summarily cast aside by the master narrative of secularization. This kind of learning is not strictly cumulative or progressive in any simple sense, however, since it takes as its point of departure a belated recognition of missed opportunities in the past. One is thus not learning from the past, so much as decentering the expectation that we occupy a superior cognitive position. This means denuding history of the scaffolding designed to guarantee distinctly modern outcomes, and is perhaps better understood as a form of unlearning, at least in the sense of foregoing specific convictions about the social-evolutionary direction of what one is doing.[7] I borrow this notion of "unlearning" from Dipesh Chakrabarty, who in his *Provincializing Europe* offers a powerful critique of historicism and invites us to "unlearn to think of history as a developmental process in which that which is possible becomes actual by tending to a future that is singular." By revising our approach to any given present, including our own, as "irreducibly not-one," we free ourselves to map out the plural possibilities at play in any present

---

6   Ibid., 17.
7   That said, it is still not yet clear how Habermas sees learning from religion, which implies a sincere and distinct effort at secular self-revision, in relation to his earlier views on the sedimentation of learning processes in social institutions, which imply a universal developmental logic. Notwithstanding Habermas's sincere commitment to learning from religious interlocutors and to allowing for different paths to modernity, it is unclear just how much his concept of the post-secular might still betoken a stadial approach to consciousness and all this entails. As more than one critic has pointed out, "the challenge … consists in finding a way to make compatible the continued presence of religion (everywhere) with the cognitive advances of modern consciousness postulated by his theory of communicative rationality" and other aspects of his social theory. See María Herrera Lima, "The Anxiety of Contingency: Religion in a Secular Age," in *Habermas and Religion*, eds., Craig Calhoun, Eduardo Mendieta, and Jonathan Van Antwerpen (New York: Polity, 2013), 50.

and break the iron grip of historicism.[8] As Chakrabarty shows so well in his analysis of political modernity in India, it is in and through the heterotemporality of the subaltern world that one can begin to fathom the way that gods and other non-human agents dwell with rather than against humans struggling to make their way in a changing world. "Although the God of monotheism may have taken a few knocks—if not actually 'died'— in the nineteenth-century European story of the 'disenchantment of the world,' the gods and other agents inhabiting practices of so-called 'superstition' have never died anywhere."[9]

Habermas is not alone in trying to rethink the continuing vitality of religion in history, and what this means for how we think about history more generally. Like Habermas, Alisdair MacIntyre took up the issue of religion midway through a career that had been framed largely by Marxism. Seeking to understand the prevailing incoherence of ethical discourse and the incommensurability of different ethical systems, MacIntyre posited that modern self-understanding rests in no small part on patterns of historical forgetting. To see this, one must discard the fiction that history itself is ever simply a neutral record of events, and admit that academic history is complicit in promoting confusion over moral discourse. "Suppose it were the case," MacIntyre asks, "that the moral and other evaluative presuppositions of academic history derived from the forms of the disorder which it brought about. Suppose, that is, that the standpoint of academic history is such that from its value-neutral viewpoint moral disorder must remain largely invisible."[10] To counter this historical forgetting, MacIntyre insists on the need to clarify one's evaluative standpoint and specify the criteria by which one judges the course of history. In stark contrast with a feigned historical neutrality that places the inquirer "above" history, affirming explicitly the criteria one uses to judge historical progress places the inquirer in a particular tradition that enables an encounter with a past that is charged with meaning. Inquiry is meaningful when it is connected to a clear understanding of the kind of life one wants to live. And the best model for this, according to

8   Dipesh Chakrabarty, *Provincializing Europe*, op. cit., 249.

9   Ibid., 16.

10 Alisdair MacIntyre, *After Virtue: A Study in Moral Theory* (New York: Bloomsbury, 2007), 4.

MacIntyre, is the Thomist conception of knowledge, shaped as it was by the deep experience of craft knowledge. On this view, the person wishing to learn something willingly submits to the authority of one who knows, a master, whose own experience serves as a model for the apprentice to imitate. By entering into a master-apprentice relationship one actively immerses oneself in a particular learning community, whose standards—whether of woodworking, weaving, or philosophizing—establish parameters that enable successive lessons to make any sense. In such a community, one comes to understand how these particular standards form a tradition that developed in one direction, and not another. One immersed in learning a craft engages the past differently

> [j]ust because at any particular moment the rationality of a craft is justified by its history so far, which has made it what it is in that specific time, place, and set of historical circumstances, such rationality is inseparable from the tradition through which it was achieved. To share in the rationality of a craft requires sharing in the contingencies of its history, understanding its story as one's own, and finding a place for oneself as a character in the enacted dramatic narrative which is that story so far. The participant in a craft is rational *qua* participant insofar as he or she conforms to the best standards of reason discovered so far, and the rationality in which he or she thus shares is always, therefore, unlike the rationality of the encyclopaedic mode, understood as a historically situated rationality, even if one which aims at a timeless formulation of its own standards which would be their final and perfected form through a series of successive reformulations, past and yet to come.[11]

Efforts to understand the past are never conducted without very specific ideas about what one hopes to find there, and so it is essential that one be clear about just what these presuppositions are and where they come from. The craft model of knowledge thus stands in contrast to the ideal of the scholar who achieves objectivity by disencumbering themselves of convictions and presuppositions. For MacIntyre, to be aware of oneself in history

11   Ibid., 65.

means understanding and affirming the political and moral stakes of historical inquiry, rather than pretending that these play no role in one's research.

Charles Taylor is another major voice to take up the question of the deep and formative imbrications of religion and history. In his monumental *A Secular Age*, Taylor criticizes those who portray secularization as so many "subtraction" stories, to wit: as a sloughing off of prejudices and outworn modes of practice and belief in a heroic commitment to letting the natural abilities of human beings flourish uninhibited. The problem with such stories, which are the stock and trade of a kind of Enlightenment humanism, broadly speaking, is that they fail to account for the emergence of new and different moral motivations in history. And for Taylor that is the story that needs to be told, namely, how society changed from one in which it was almost impossible not to believe in God to one in which such a belief was only one among many options. This transition involved much more than turning on "the lights" of reason and satirizing the moral hypocrisy of the clergy, and Taylor offers a deft analysis of the complex and shifting conditions surrounding belief and unbelief between 1500 and 2000. Building on his earlier *Sources of the Self* and *Modern Social Imaginaries*, he sketches a process of "disembedding" whereby individuals are increasingly "buffered" against all manner of entanglement with spirits and supernatural forces in the world, and hence experience and conceptualize the world in new ways. Inured against these forces, the buffered self takes on the burden of discipline and self-control, and deploys these in a way that carves out an interiorized sense of self that relates to all other individuals on a similar basis. This interiorization occurs in tandem with a decoupling of the natural world from any reference to a transcendent order, the upshot of which is that the modern world offers the possibility of living and interpreting life according to a purely immanent frame of reference. But in spite of this increased power, the buffered self cannot dispense with history; according to Taylor "it is a crucial fact of our present spiritual predicament that it is historical; that is, our understanding of ourselves and where we stand is partly defined by our sense of having come to where we are, of having overcome a previous condition." The widespread use of "disenchanted" to describe the modern world might be insufficient as a descriptor of complex historical processes, but it is not merely a rubric that can be corrected. The expression itself must be viewed from within, as an expression of existential orientation:

> … [W]e are widely aware of living in a "disenchanted" universe; and the use of this word bespeaks our sense that it was once enchanted. More, we are not only aware that it used to be so, but also that it was a struggle and an achievement to get where we are, and that in some respects this achievement is fragile. We know this because each one of us as we grew up has had to take on the disciplines of disenchantment, and we regularly reproach each other for our failings in this regard, and accuse each other of "magical" thinking, of indulging in "myth," of giving way to "fantasy"; we say that X isn't living in our century, that Y has a "medieval" mind, while Z, whom we admire, is way ahead of her time.[12]

Though the standard story of secularization might "misdescribe it grievously by misidentifying the itinerary," the story cannot be dispensed with, because "[o]ur past is sedimented in our present, and we are doomed to misidentify ourselves as long as we can't do justice to where we come from."[13]

These are not the only attempts at a frank settling of accounts with modern assumptions about religion, but they have been influential, helping to prompt a complex debate over whether and how scholars might cultivate a post-secular approach. The debate is many-sided, and there are a variety of ways that one might construe or condemn what post-secular means. In a useful attempt to summarize the debate, James Beckford has catalogued six clusters of meaning surrounding how post-secular is used by different authors.[14] In a similar vein, Justin Beaumont, Klaus Eder, and Eduardo Mendieta offer five rubrics for categorizing different ways post-secular is deployed methodologically. Both approaches are illuminating in their own

12 Charles Taylor, *A Secular Age*, op. cit., 28–29.
13 Ibid., 29.
14 James Beckford, "SSSR Presidential Address Public Religions and the Post-secular: Critical Reflections," in *Journal for the Scientific Study of Religion* 51:1 (2012): 1–19.

way, and offer important possibilities for making sense of the rapidly growing literature on the topic. But it is worth noting that these inventories,
though certainly mindful of the role of secularization and its attendant notions as factors in history, do not take the full measure of the generative
role that thinking about religion has played in establishing the distinctive
historico-temporal self-understanding of modernity as an epochal mode of
consciousness—not only in and through what it thinks and says about itself
and others, but how it distributes thinking in time and as time. Modernity
is the authority to discriminate between ideas that do and don't belong,
and to place ideas in their appropriate time. In this Newtonian universe,
space and time are absolute coordinates, operating independently of each
other and any observer, and policed by the enactment of prohibitions
against anachronism and repetition in history. But like all "post" formula-
tions, post-secular remains beholden to an epochal consciousness that, no
matter how attenuated, is no less modern for seeking an honest reckoning
about the place of religion in the modern world. And it will never achieve
a sincere "self-confrontation" or "the enactment of reflexive secularization"
if it does not forego its commitment to this schema of absolute coordinates
and be open to the possibility that it is when the center cannot hold that
one stands on the edge of a truly different reality.[15] The task that confronts
us is not to demolish theories of secularization in the name of another overcoming; for doing so would involve the same kind of triumphalist historicism endemic to these theories, whose template has in many ways been
secularization. The task, rather, is to frame an approach to history that ex-
pands how we understand the great variety of past events and ways of living,
living with, and without, and around gods and other spiritualities. The task
is to frame an approach to history that enables—rather than denies—coevalness with the full range of human experience, as possibilities that may
yet, may still, and may always, remain for us.

15 Justin Beaumont, Klaus Eder, and Eduardo Mendieta, "'Reflexive Seculariza-
    tion' Concepts, Processes, and Antagonisms of Postsecularity," in *European
    Journal of Social Theory* 23.3 (2018): 9.